A History of Ethiopia

John Galea

Table of Contents

- **Introduction**
- **Chapter 1** The Cradle of Humankind: Prehistoric Ethiopia
- **Chapter 2** The Land of Punt and the Rise of D'mt
- **Chapter 3** The Aksumite Empire: A Global Trading Power.
- **Chapter 4** The Embrace of Christianity and the Golden Age of Aksum
- **Chapter 5** The Zagwe Dynasty and the Rock-Hewn Churches of Lalibela
- **Chapter 6** The Solomonic Restoration and Imperial Expansion.
- **Chapter 7** The Ethiopian-Adal War and the Portuguese Intervention (1529–1543).
- **Chapter 8** The Gondarine Period: Castles and Cultural Renaissance
- **Chapter 9** Zemene Mesafint: The Era of Princes and Warlords
- **Chapter 10** The Rise of a Unifier: Emperor Tewodros II.
- **Chapter 11** The Reign of Yohannes IV: Defending the Faith and the Nation
- **Chapter 12** Emperor Menelik II and the Scramble for Africa
- **Chapter 13** The Battle of Adwa: An African Victory.

- **Chapter 14** The Early Reign of Haile Selassie: Modernization and Centralization.

- **Chapter 15** The Italian Invasion and Occupation (1935–1941).

- **Chapter 16** Liberation and the Return of the Emperor

- **Chapter 17** The Post-War Years and the Federation with Eritrea.

- **Chapter 18** The Twilight of the Monarchy: Social Unrest and Famine

- **Chapter 19** The 1974 Revolution and the Rise of the Derg.

- **Chapter 20** The Red Terror and the Ethiopian Civil War.

- **Chapter 21** The Fall of the Derg and the Transitional Government

- **Chapter 22** The Federal Democratic Republic: A New Constitution.

- **Chapter 23** Conflict and Tensions: The Ethio-Eritrean War (1998-2000).

- **Chapter 24** Ethiopia in the 21st Century: Growth, Challenges, and Transformation

- **Chapter 25** The 2020 Civil War and the Quest for a Lasting Peace.

Introduction

Ethiopia, a land of dramatic landscapes and ancient civilizations, presents a history as rich and complex as any on Earth. It is a story that begins at the dawn of humankind itself, in the Rift Valley where the fossilized remains of our earliest ancestors, including the famed "Lucy," were unearthed. This legacy as the cradle of humanity is but the first chapter in a narrative that spans millennia, encompassing the rise and fall of powerful empires, the enduring influence of ancient faiths, and a remarkable history of independence on a continent largely shaped by colonial rule.

The historical tapestry of Ethiopia is woven with the threads of powerful kingdoms that left an indelible mark on the region and the world. The mysterious kingdom of D'mt, which emerged in the 10th century BC, stands as one of the earliest known civilizations in this territory. It was succeeded by the formidable Aksumite Empire, which rose to prominence in the 1st century AD. From its capital in the northern highlands, Aksum became a major player in the commercial networks linking the Roman Empire with ancient India, trading in ivory, gold, and spices. The Aksumites developed their own written script, Ge'ez, and minted their own currency, a testament to their economic and political might. A pivotal moment in Aksumite and Ethiopian history occurred in the 4th century AD with the conversion of King Ezana to Christianity, establishing one of the oldest Christian traditions in the world.

Following the decline of Aksum, due in part to the rise of Islam and shifting trade routes, power shifted south. The Zagwe dynasty emerged, leaving behind an extraordinary legacy in the rock-hewn churches of Lalibela. These remarkable monolithic structures, carved directly out of the volcanic rock, were conceived as a "New Jerusalem" and remain a vibrant center of pilgrimage and worship to this day. The Zagwe were in turn succeeded by the Solomonic dynasty in the 13th century, which claimed direct descent from the biblical King Solomon and the Queen of Sheba. This lineage, chronicled in the epic *Kebra Nagast*, would form a cornerstone of

Ethiopian national identity and imperial legitimacy for over 700 years.

The medieval and early modern periods were characterized by imperial expansion, cultural flourishing, and significant challenges. The Ethiopian Empire consolidated its power in the Horn of Africa, but also faced external threats, most notably from the Adal Sultanate in the 16th century. This conflict, which drew in the Portuguese, marked a period of intense religious and political struggle.

A defining feature of Ethiopia's more recent history is its successful resistance against European colonialism. During the late 19th-century "Scramble for Africa," while the rest of the continent was being partitioned by European powers, Ethiopia maintained its sovereignty. The crowning achievement of this resistance was the decisive victory over Italian forces at the Battle of Adwa in 1896, under the leadership of Emperor Menelik II. This victory resonated across Africa and the African diaspora, becoming a powerful symbol of black freedom and resistance.

The 20th century brought both modernization and immense turmoil. The reign of Emperor Haile Selassie I saw efforts to centralize the state and introduce reforms, but was also marked by the brutal Italian invasion and occupation from 1935 to 1941. Following the restoration of independence, Ethiopia played a significant role in the pan-African movement. However, internal pressures, including famine and social unrest, led to the overthrow of the monarchy in 1974.

The revolution ushered in a period of radical change under a Marxist-Leninist military junta known as the Derg. This era was defined by sweeping land reforms, nationalization, and the brutal "Red Terror," a campaign of violence against political opponents that resulted in widespread human rights abuses. The Derg's rule was also beset by civil war, particularly in Eritrea and Tigray, and devastating famines.

The fall of the Derg in 1991 marked another turning point, leading to the establishment of a transitional government and eventually the Federal Democratic Republic of Ethiopia. The subsequent decades have been a period of significant economic growth and transformation, but also of persistent challenges, including ethnic tensions, political conflict, and the devastating Ethio-Eritrean War of 1998-2000. The 21st century has seen Ethiopia navigate the complexities of development, democracy, and regional stability, culminating in the recent civil war that began in 2020. This book seeks to explore this long and multifaceted history, from its deepest origins to its contemporary struggles and triumphs, providing a comprehensive account of one of the world's most fascinating and enduring nations.

CHAPTER ONE: The Cradle of Humankind: Prehistoric Ethiopia

To begin the story of Ethiopia is to begin the story of humanity itself. The narrative is not etched in ancient texts or carved on monuments, but rather fossilized in the very bedrock of the land. For millions of years, the unique geology of the Great Rift Valley, a massive tear in the Earth's crust that runs through the heart of the country, has created the perfect conditions for preserving the fragile remains of our most distant ancestors. This vast, tectonically active region has acted as a patient archivist, burying bones in layers of sediment and volcanic ash, only to expose them again millennia later through the slow, persistent work of erosion. It is within this dramatic landscape, particularly in the sun-scorched Afar Depression, that paleoanthropologists have unearthed a sequential story of human evolution, earning Ethiopia its unparalleled title: the Cradle of Humankind.

The tale starts long before the appearance of beings recognizably human. Around 4.4 million years ago, a creature known as *Ardipithecus ramidus* roamed the woodlands of what is now Ethiopia's Middle Awash region. First discovered by a team led by American paleoanthropologist Tim White between 1992 and 1994, the species became widely known through a remarkably complete partial skeleton nicknamed "Ardi." The analysis of Ardi, a female of the species, was a monumental undertaking, finally published in detail in 2009. Her skeleton was a mosaic of primitive and advanced features; it suggested a creature comfortable both in the trees and on the ground. While possessing a grasping big toe useful for climbing, other aspects of her pelvis and feet indicated an ability to walk upright on two legs, a hallmark of the hominin lineage. Ardi's world was not the open savanna once thought to be the exclusive driver of bipedalism, but a woodland environment, challenging long-held theories about why our ancestors first stood up.

Over a million years after Ardi, the Ethiopian landscape was home to one of the most famous and pivotal species in the human family tree: *Australopithecus afarensis*. This species, which lived from roughly 3.9 to 2.9 million years ago, is known from several hundred fossil specimens found in East Africa. The most celebrated of these is AL 288-1, a 40 percent complete skeleton of a female discovered in 1974 at Hadar in the Afar region by a team including Donald Johanson. She was given the name "Lucy," inspired by a Beatles song played repeatedly in the celebration camp that evening. Lucy, who stood just over a meter tall, had a small, ape-like skull but a pelvis and leg bones that were astonishingly human-like, providing definitive proof that bipedalism was well-established long before the evolution of large brains.

The picture of *Australopithecus afarensis* was further enriched by another extraordinary find in 2000, not far from where Lucy was unearthed. A team led by Ethiopian paleoanthropologist Zeresenay Alemseged discovered the fossilized remains of a three-year-old female of the same species in the Dikika region. Nicknamed "Selam," meaning "peace" in Amharic, this 3.3-million-year-old fossil was even more complete than Lucy's and provided an unprecedented glimpse into the childhood of our ancient relatives. Selam's skeleton, including a nearly complete skull, torso, and limbs, confirmed the species' dual aptitude for walking upright on the ground and climbing in trees. Her gorilla-like shoulder blades and long, curved fingers were clear adaptations for an arboreal life, suggesting that for these early hominins, the forest remained a vital source of food and a refuge from predators.

The story of human evolution is not merely about changing skeletons; it is also about the dawn of technology. For millennia, our ancestors used unmodified stones or sticks, much like modern chimpanzees do. However, a significant cognitive leap occurred when they began to intentionally fracture stones to create sharp edges for cutting, scraping, and butchering. For a long time, the oldest known examples of this systematic tool production, known as the Oldowan industry, were dated to between 2.58 and 2.55 million years ago at Gona, Ethiopia. But in 2019, an even older site, Bokol Dora 1, also in Ethiopia's Afar region, pushed back the origins of this technology. Excavations there revealed a trove of flaked stone tools dated to older than 2.58 million years ago, representing the earliest known evidence for the widespread production of Oldowan tools.

These early toolmakers were taking a crucial step. Instead of simply using a rock to hammer something, they were demonstrating the foresight and skill to turn one rock into another, more useful object. This technological shift appears to have happened around the same time that the genus *Homo* first emerged. Indeed, the Bokol Dora 1 site is near Ledi-Geraru, where the oldest known fossil attributed to our genus, a 2.8-million-year-old jawbone, was discovered. The appearance of toolmaking and the emergence of *Homo* in the same region at roughly the same time suggests a powerful link between technological innovation and the evolution of our own lineage. Recent discoveries of fossil teeth at Ledi-Geraru even indicate that early *Homo* and a species of *Australopithecus* co-existed in the region between 2.8 and 2.6 million years ago, painting a complex picture of a diverse hominin landscape.

As hominins evolved, so did their technology. Following the simple choppers and flakes of the Oldowan, a more sophisticated tool kit known as the Acheulean industry emerged. The hallmark of this tradition was the bifacial hand-axe, a teardrop-shaped tool carefully worked on both sides to produce a sharp, durable edge. This more standardized and deliberately shaped tool reflects a significant advance in cognitive ability, planning, and manufacturing skill. One of the most important sites for understanding this period in Ethiopia is Melka Kunture, located about 50 kilometers south of modern-day Addis Ababa. First discovered in 1963, this vast, open-air site contains a remarkably long and continuous archaeological record, with layers of sediment preserving evidence of hominin activity spanning well over a million years.

The extensive excavations at Melka Kunture have unearthed numerous Acheulean hand-axes, alongside the fossilized remains of the hominins who made them, including *Homo erectus*. The site, which was situated along the banks of the Awash River, seems to have been occupied repeatedly over immense spans of time, with hominins drawn to its reliable water source and the raw materials available for toolmaking. The layers at Melka Kunture show a gradual refinement of Acheulean technology over hundreds of thousands of years, providing a unique window into the developing minds and capabilities of our ancestors. The site is a testament to the enduring presence of early humans in the Ethiopian highlands, adapting to changing environments and honing the skills that would eventually allow them to spread across the globe.

After a long reign of *Homo erectus* and the Acheulean tradition, the next major chapter in human prehistory saw the emergence of our own species, *Homo sapiens*. Once again, the fossil record of Ethiopia provides the most crucial evidence for this evolutionary transition. For decades, the debate over human origins centered on whether modern humans evolved in one place—Africa—before spreading out (the "Out of Africa" model) or evolved simultaneously in different regions of the world from existing hominin populations (the "Multiregional" model). Discoveries in Ethiopia have provided overwhelming support for the former.

In the late 1960s, a team led by Richard Leakey discovered fossilized skulls at a site called Omo Kibish in the southwestern Omo Valley. These remains, known as Omo I and Omo II, were recognized as anatomically modern *Homo sapiens*. For years, their precise age was uncertain, but was thought to be less than 200,000 years old. However, recent advances in dating techniques, specifically by analyzing the layers of volcanic ash above and below where the fossils were found, have pushed back their age significantly. The Omo I fossils are now considered to be at least 230,000 years old, making them the oldest undisputed remains of *Homo sapiens* ever discovered. The skull of Omo I possesses unequivocally modern human features, such as a tall, globular braincase and a prominent chin, cementing its status as the earliest known member of our species.

This evidence was powerfully supplemented by a discovery made in 1997 near the village of Herto in the Middle Awash region. There, researchers found three fossilized crania—two adults and one child—that were radioisotopically dated to between 160,000 and 154,000 years ago. These skulls, assigned to the subspecies *Homo sapiens idaltu*, are morphologically intermediate between older, more archaic African hominins and fully modern humans. They are robust, with large brain volumes, but lack the distinctive features of Neanderthals, their European contemporaries. The Herto skulls filled a major gap in the fossil record and provided a clear picture of what our immediate ancestors looked like, further solidifying the case for an African origin for all humanity. Intriguingly, cut marks on the child's skull and one of the adult skulls suggest they were deliberately handled after death, hinting at some form of ancient mortuary practice.

The period in which these early *Homo sapiens* lived is known as the Middle Stone Age (MSA). This era was characterized by a significant leap in technological and behavioral complexity. The large, cumbersome hand-axes of the Acheulean were replaced by more sophisticated toolkits. MSA toolmakers developed techniques like the Levallois method, which involved carefully preparing a stone core to strike off flakes of a predetermined size and shape. This allowed for the efficient production of specialized tools like points, which could be hafted onto spears, and scrapers for processing hides.

Numerous MSA sites have been identified across Ethiopia, from the Rift Valley to the highlands. The Gademotta Formation, west of Lake Ziway, contains one of the oldest MSA sites in Africa, with evidence of stone-tipped throwing spears dating back over 279,000 years. This indicates that the technological innovations of the MSA may have predated the appearance of the first anatomically modern humans. Other important sites, such as those in the Aduma region of the Middle Awash, show that MSA populations were highly adaptable, exploiting a variety of environments, including riverine habitats where they hunted large fish. The discovery of a rock shelter at Fincha Habera in the Bale Mountains, used by MSA people some 30,000 years ago at an altitude of over 11,000 feet, demonstrates the remarkable ability of our ancestors to adapt to even the most challenging high-altitude environments.

The final phase of the Stone Age, the Later Stone Age (LSA), saw further refinement in tool technology, with a trend towards miniaturization. The production of small, standardized stone blades, or microliths, which could be set into bone or wooden handles to create composite tools like barbed arrows, became widespread. While the prehistoric record in Ethiopia from this period is less complete, the transition represents a continued pattern of innovation. It is also during this broader prehistoric period that the first stirrings of symbolic thought and art appear. While Ethiopia does not have the extensive Paleolithic cave paintings of Europe, it is rich in rock art from later periods. In the eastern region of Hararghe and in the south, numerous rock shelters and caves are adorned with paintings and engravings. These images, mostly depicting cattle and other animals, as well as human figures, belong to a more recent prehistoric past, likely dating from the 3rd millennium BC onwards, but they represent a vital connection to the deep artistic and cultural roots of the region's people. This artistic expression, coupled with the long record of technological advancement and physical evolution preserved in the fossil record, completes the opening chapter of Ethiopia's unparalleled human story.

CHAPTER TWO: The Land of Punt and the Rise of D'mt

Long before the great stelae of Aksum pierced the sky, and even before the first stones of Rome were laid, the northern highlands of Ethiopia and the adjoining Red Sea coast were entangled in the grand commerce and mythology of the ancient world. The story of this era unfolds from two distinct but overlapping perspectives: one looking outward from the powerful civilization of Pharaonic Egypt, which chronicled its ambitious expeditions to a semi-mythical land of riches, and the other emerging from the Ethiopian soil itself, with the rise of the earliest known kingdom in the region. This chapter navigates the hazy frontier between the Late Bronze Age and the Iron Age, exploring the celebrated Land of Punt and the formidable, yet enigmatic, kingdom of D'mt.

For the ancient Egyptians, the world to their south was a source of exotic and essential goods. While Nubia was a known, and often subjugated, source of gold and soldiers, further beyond lay a more mysterious realm they called Punt. In their texts, they also referred to it as *Ta Netjer*, the "Land of the God," suggesting it was a place of divine origins, perhaps even the ancestral homeland of some of their deities. For over a thousand years, from the Old Kingdom to the New Kingdom, the journey to Punt represented the pinnacle of Egyptian long-distance trade. The earliest recorded expedition was dispatched by Pharaoh Sahure in the 25th century BC, but Egyptian records indicate that gold from Punt was present in the kingdom even earlier, during the reign of Khufu, the builder of the Great Pyramid.

The allure of Punt lay in its extraordinary natural wealth. Egyptian ships braved the treacherous waters of the Red Sea not for conquest, but for commerce in luxury items that were indispensable for the religious and courtly life of the pharaohs. The most precious of these were the aromatic resins, myrrh and frankincense, which were burned in vast quantities as incense in temple rituals. Beyond the sacred perfumes, Punt provided a bounty of other treasures: ebony and other rare woods, gold, ivory, leopard skins, and a menagerie of live animals, including giraffes, leopards, and, most prized of all, hamadryas baboons, which were sacred to the god Thoth.

The most vivid and detailed account of this trade comes from the reign of one of Egypt's most remarkable rulers, the female pharaoh Hatshepsut. Around 1470 BC, she commissioned a major seafaring expedition to Punt. The story of this voyage is not confined to dusty papyrus scrolls but is spectacularly carved in detailed bas-reliefs on the walls of her mortuary temple at Deir el-Bahri, near modern Luxor. These carvings offer an unparalleled window into the world of Punt. We see a fleet of five large, oared ships, each seventy feet long, being loaded with Egyptian goods for trade, including beer, wine, and jewelry. The expedition was led by a high official named Nehsi and was escorted by a contingent of marines, suggesting that while the mission was peaceful, it was not without its risks.

The reliefs depict the Egyptians' arrival in a lush, exotic land. The Puntites are shown living in distinctive beehive-shaped houses raised on stilts, accessed by ladders, and surrounded by palm and myrrh trees. The carvings introduce us to the rulers of Punt at that time, a chief named Perehu and his wife, Ati. Perehu is depicted as a typical man of high status, while his wife is shown with a pronounced curvature of the spine and large rolls of fat on her limbs, a unique portrayal that has sparked endless debate among scholars, with some suggesting she may have had a condition like elephantiasis. The encounter appears to be one of amicable diplomacy and trade. The Egyptians present their goods, and the Puntites, in turn, offer their treasures. The most remarkable scene shows the Egyptians carefully digging up live myrrh trees, their root balls wrapped in baskets, to be transplanted in the soil of Egypt—the first recorded attempt at transplanting foreign flora.

The triumphant return of the expedition is depicted with great fanfare. The ships are shown heavily laden with all the produce of Punt, including the precious myrrh trees and troops of baboons clambering in the rigging. This successful mission was a major propaganda victory for Hatshepsut, reinforcing her legitimacy and demonstrating her ability to bring divine blessings and immense prosperity to Egypt. But for all the detail in these magnificent reliefs, they omit one crucial piece of information: a map. The exact location of Punt has been one of the great enduring mysteries of ancient history, debated by scholars for over 150 years.

The general consensus has long placed Punt somewhere in the southern Red Sea region, but the precise area has been contested. Candidates have included the coasts of modern-day Sudan, Eritrea, Ethiopia, Djibouti, and Somalia, with some even suggesting it spanned both the African Horn and southern Arabia. The wildlife and products depicted in Hatshepsut's reliefs, especially the giraffes and myrrh trees, strongly point to an African location. In recent years, scientific analysis has provided a powerful new line of evidence. Researchers studying the chemical isotopes in the hair and bones of mummified baboons brought from Punt and preserved in Egyptian tombs were able to match their geographic origins. The results pointed not to Somalia or Yemen, but squarely to a region encompassing modern-day Eritrea and parts of eastern Ethiopia. This evidence strongly suggests that the legendary Land of the Gods, the source of Egypt's most valued exotic goods, was located in the northern territory of the future Ethiopian state.

While the Egyptians were documenting their coastal voyages to Punt, a new and powerful society was beginning to coalesce in the highlands of that same region. Emerging around the 8th century BC, this kingdom is known to history as D'mt. It represents the first major state-level society, the first great indigenous civilization to arise in the Ethiopian highlands. For many years, the story of D'mt was told as a tale of colonization. The striking similarities in architecture, religion, and writing between D'mt and the powerful Sabean kingdom of modern-day Yemen led early scholars to conclude that D'mt was little more than a Sabean colonial outpost, established to control trade routes from the African interior.

This "colonial" model, however, has been largely revised by modern archaeology. While the South Arabian influence is undeniable, the evidence now points to D'mt being a thoroughly

African kingdom that engaged in a dynamic cultural exchange with its neighbors across the Red Sea. Rather than a colony, it was a local polity that adopted and brilliantly adapted foreign ideas and technologies to its own purposes. Archaeological data now suggests that complex societies were already developing in the region before the period of intense Sabean contact, indicating that foreign influences were grafted onto a robust, pre-existing indigenous culture. South Arabian migrants, likely traders, craftspeople, and perhaps some elites, did cross the sea, but they appear to have integrated into the local population, creating a unique cultural fusion.

The heartland of the D'mt kingdom was in the area of modern-day Tigray in northern Ethiopia and adjacent parts of Eritrea. Its capital is believed to have been at Yeha, a site that still holds the most impressive architectural relic of this era. Here, a magnificent structure known as the Great Temple of Yeha still stands, a testament to the skill of D'mt's builders. Constructed around the 7th century BC, the temple is a rectangular tower built of large, precisely cut limestone blocks fitted together without mortar, a technique characteristic of Sabean masonry. The sheer quality of its construction is the reason for its remarkable state of preservation over 2,600 years. The temple was dedicated to Almaqah, the principal deity of the Sabean pantheon, a god associated with the moon and agriculture. The presence of his temple at Yeha is the most potent symbol of the cultural currents flowing across the Red Sea during this period.

The Sabean influence is also clearly visible in the writing system used by the D'mt elite. They adopted the Epigraphic South Arabian script, an elegant alphabet of consonants, to write both their own language and the Sabean of the newcomers. Inscriptions found at Yeha and other sites name several early rulers, though the records are too sparse to construct a detailed political history. Alongside Almaqah, the D'mt pantheon included a mix of other South Arabian and indigenous deities, again highlighting the hybrid nature of their culture.

The economy of D'mt was likely based on the fertile soils of the highlands. These early agropastoral peoples used plows, grew millet, and developed irrigation schemes to enhance their agricultural productivity. They also possessed the technology of iron working, producing tools and weapons. Strategically positioned, the rulers of D'mt were also able to control the lucrative trade routes leading from the interior of Africa to the Red Sea coast. The same goods that had drawn the Egyptians to Punt for centuries—ivory, gold, incense, and obsidian—would have passed through D'mt territory, providing a significant source of wealth and power for its elite.

Despite its impressive beginnings, the history of D'mt after the 5th century BC becomes murky. The kingdom appears to have declined, and the centralized state fragmented. The precise reasons for this decline are unknown. It may have been linked to the waning power of its main trading partner, the Sabean kingdom in Yemen. As Saba's influence in the region faded, the cultural ties across the Red Sea weakened, and the elite culture of D'mt appears to have become more distinctly African. The South Arabian script and religious practices gradually disappeared, evolving into proto-Ge'ez and local forms of worship.

Following the fall of D'mt, the northern plateau was not a political vacuum but rather a landscape of smaller, successor kingdoms. This "pre-Aksumite" transitional period is poorly understood due to a lack of inscriptions and limited archaeological work. It appears to have been a time of political decentralization, with multiple smaller polities and city-states, like Yeha, Matara, and a nascent Aksum, vying for influence. Out of this crucible of competing powers, one would eventually rise to reunite the region and build an empire that would dwarf D'mt in scale and influence. The foundations of Ethiopian civilization, however, had been firmly laid. The legacy of Punt had established the region as a vital node in international trade networks, while D'mt had demonstrated the potential for a powerful, centralized state to emerge in the Ethiopian highlands, creating a unique synthesis of indigenous African culture and sophisticated technologies from the wider world.

CHAPTER THREE: The Aksumite Empire: A Global Trading Power

Out of the fragmented landscape of post-D'mt kingdoms, a new, formidable power began to assert itself around the 1st century AD. Centered on the town of Aksum in the Tigray highlands, this burgeoning state would not only unify the region but would also build an empire whose influence stretched across the Red Sea and deep into the African interior. This was the Aksumite Empire, a civilization whose wealth and power were built not on isolation, but on a sophisticated and aggressive engagement with the wider world. Its rise marked a pivotal moment, transforming the Horn of Africa from a peripheral supplier of exotic goods into the home of a major player in the grand economic theater that linked the Roman Empire with ancient India.

The earliest detailed glimpse of this rising kingdom comes not from an Aksumite source, but from the logbook of an anonymous Greco-Roman merchant. The *Periplus of the Erythraean Sea*, a 1st-century AD trade manual, describes the sea lanes and markets from Roman Egypt to the coast of India. The author provides a vivid snapshot of the Aksumite coast, noting the port of Adulis as a bustling hub for the ivory trade. He then describes an eight-day overland journey from the coast to the "metropolis... which is called Axomites." There, he writes, ruled a king named Zoscales, a man who was not only in charge but also "acquainted with Greek literature," a telling detail that reveals Aksum's early integration into the cultural and commercial currents of the Mediterranean world.

The engine of Aksum's prosperity was its strategic geography. The empire was perfectly positioned to control two immensely valuable economic zones: the fertile highlands, which provided agricultural surplus and a strong population base, and the Red Sea coast, the primary artery for international maritime trade. At the heart of this commercial network was the port of Adulis. Situated on the Eritrean coast, Adulis became the premier gateway for goods flowing out of Africa and for the manufactured products of the Roman and Indian worlds flowing in. Excavations at the site have revealed a cosmopolitan city with impressive stone buildings, including early Christian churches, and artifacts linking it to Egypt, the Mediterranean, and beyond.

From the African interior, Aksumite merchants funneled a fortune in luxury goods to the docks of Adulis. The most significant of these was ivory, a commodity in high demand throughout the ancient world for carving, inlay, and ornamentation. The *Periplus* notes that all the ivory from the lands beyond the Nile was brought to Aksum before being sent to the coast. Alongside ivory, Aksum exported tortoise shells, rhinoceros horn, gold, emeralds, and incense. The empire also participated in the slave trade, a common and brutal feature of ancient economies. In return, ships from the Roman Empire arrived laden with dyed cloth, glassware, wine and olive oil from Italy and Syria, and metal goods like copper and iron tools. From the east came spices, silk, and cotton textiles from India, demonstrating Aksum's crucial role as a middleman connecting the great empires of the age.

This dramatic expansion of trade was fueled by a major shift in maritime technology around the 1st century AD. Sailors learned to harness the seasonal monsoon winds to make direct open-sea crossings of the Arabian Sea, bypassing the slower and more dangerous coastal routes. This innovation supercharged the trade between the Roman world and India, and Aksum, with its powerful navy and control of the Red Sea choke points, was ideally placed to profit from the increased traffic. The kingdom grew rich by taxing this trade and by dominating the supply of African luxury goods that the Romans, Persians, and Indians so desperately craved.

In a move that powerfully symbolized its sovereignty and economic sophistication, Aksum became one of the first African polities to mint its own currency. Starting around 270 AD under a king named Endubis, Aksumite rulers began issuing beautiful and precisely weighted coins in gold, silver, and bronze. This was an act of immense political significance, a declaration that Aksum considered itself an equal to the great coin-issuing empires like Rome and Persia. The earliest coins were intended for international trade, struck to the weight standard of the Roman Empire and inscribed in Greek to ensure their acceptance in foreign markets. These pre-Christian coins bore a portrait of the king, typically wearing a distinctive crown or headcloth, and were marked with the pagan crescent-and-disk symbol, representing deities shared with South Arabian traditions. The reverse of the coins was often framed by two stalks of barley or teff, a clear statement of the agricultural wealth that underpinned the empire's commercial might.

The wealth generated by trade financed a powerful state and a formidable military. The Aksumite government was a monarchy, ruled by a king who bore the title *Negus*, and later *Negusa Nagast*, or "King of Kings," indicating his lordship over a confederation of smaller, tributary kingdoms. The capital city, Aksum, grew into a major urban center with grand palaces and elite residences. Typical Aksumite monumental architecture involved stone walls interspersed with wooden beams, all resting on high, stepped granite platforms. The society was hierarchical, with the king and nobles at the top, followed by merchants, artisans, and a large population of farmers who cultivated the highlands, growing crops like teff and wheat.

The most dramatic expression of royal power and engineering prowess was the carving and erection of giant granite stelae, or obelisks, to mark the tombs of the rulers and nobility. Quarried from sites several kilometers away, these single-stone monoliths were transported and erected using what must have been an immense and highly organized labor force. The largest of these, the Great Stele, stood an astonishing 33 meters high and weighed over 500 tons, making it one of the largest single blocks of stone ever shaped and erected in the ancient world. It unfortunately fell during or shortly after its erection, but others remain standing. Many of the stelae are intricately carved with false doors and windows, mimicking the appearance of multi-story Aksumite buildings and serving as symbolic houses for the deceased in the afterlife. These silent stone giants remain a powerful testament to the ambition and resources of the Aksumite kings.

Aksum's commercial and military might earned it a place on the world stage. By the 3rd century AD, its power was so widely recognized that the Persian prophet Mani, founder of the Manichaean religion, named Aksum as one of the four great kingdoms of the world, alongside Rome, Persia, and China. This was not empty flattery; it was a sober assessment of global power. Aksum was not content to merely control trade routes; it actively projected its power across the Red Sea. Throughout the 3rd century, Aksumite kings like GDRT and 'DBH launched military expeditions into South Arabia, vying with the local Himyarite and Sabean kingdoms for control of the lucrative trade on the other side of the sea. For a time, Aksum controlled significant territory in Yemen, styling its rulers as kings of both Aksum and Himyar.

To its south and west, Aksum also expanded its influence. The empire inherited and eventually eclipsed its old rival, the Kingdom of Kush. By the 2nd and 3rd centuries, Aksum controlled territory previously held by the Kushites and diverted the flow of ivory from the Nile Valley through its own port of Adulis. This expansion culminated in the 4th century under King Ezana, who, even before his famous conversion to Christianity, launched a major campaign deep into Nubia. In a detailed inscription, Ezana records his decisive victory over the Noba people and the final subjugation of the remnants of the Kushite kingdom at Meroë, boasting that he had established a throne in their capital.

The pre-Christian culture of Aksum was a unique blend of its African roots and influences from across the Red Sea. The people practiced a polytheistic religion, worshipping a pantheon of gods that included Astar (a Venus deity), the war god Mahrem, from whom the kings claimed their descent, and Beher, an earth god. These deities were a continuation of earlier South Arabian traditions but had taken on a distinctly Aksumite character. The written language of the elite was Ge'ez, an indigenous Semitic language with its own unique script that evolved from the South Arabian alphabet. While Greek was used for international commerce on the gold coinage, Ge'ez was the language of the court and, eventually, the church, becoming a foundational element of Ethiopian identity.

By the early 4th century, the Aksumite Empire stood at the zenith of its power as a trading giant and a regional superpower. Its cities were prosperous, its armies were victorious, and its merchants sailed the sea lanes from the shores of Egypt to the coast of Sri Lanka. The kingdom had forged a complex and confident identity, built on its deep African heritage and its dynamic engagement with the great civilizations of the age. But the reign of its greatest pre-Christian king, Ezana, would witness a profound transformation, a spiritual revolution that would realign the empire's destiny and shape the future of the nation for millennia to come.

CHAPTER FOUR: The Embrace of Christianity and the Golden Age of Aksum

In the early 4th century, the Aksumite Empire stood at the apex of its power, a confident pagan kingdom whose merchants commanded the sea lanes and whose armies were the terror of its neighbors. Its great stelae pointed to the sky, honoring rulers who claimed descent from the war god Mahrem. But a profound transformation was underway, a spiritual revolution that would not only reshape the empire's soul but also realign its geopolitical destiny. This change came not through conquest or coercion, but through a chance shipwreck and the quiet influence of two young Syrian boys, culminating in Aksum's embrace of Christianity and the dawn of a new golden age.

The traditional story of this pivotal moment is preserved in the writings of the 4th-century church historian Tyrannius Rufinus, who heard it directly from one of the participants. Sometime in the early 300s, a Christian philosopher from Tyre named Meropius set out on a voyage to India, taking two young relatives with him, Frumentius and Aedesius. On their return journey, their ship docked at an Aksumite port on the Red Sea. A local dispute erupted, the treaty between Aksum and the Romans having been recently broken, and the ship was attacked. Everyone on board was killed, except for the two boys, who were found studying under a tree. Spared because of their youth, they were taken to the capital and presented as slaves to the king, Ella Amida.

The king, recognizing their intelligence and education, soon appointed them to positions of trust within the court. Aedesius became the royal cupbearer, while the elder and more capable Frumentius was made the king's treasurer and secretary. Before his death, the king granted them their freedom, but the widowed queen, Sofya, prevailed upon them to stay and tutor her young son and heir, Ezana. During the prince's minority, Frumentius effectively acted as regent, using his position of influence to support the growing community of Roman Christian merchants in

Aksum. He encouraged them to practice their faith openly and helped them establish places of worship, laying the groundwork for the religion to take root in the kingdom.

When King Ezana came of age, Aedesius returned home to Tyre, but Frumentius had a grander mission in mind. Convinced that Aksum was ready for a more organized church, he traveled not home, but to the great theological center of Alexandria in Egypt. There, he presented himself to the formidable Patriarch, Athanasius, and requested that a bishop be sent to shepherd the fledgling Christian community in Aksum. According to Rufinus, Athanasius convened a council of priests, and after considering Frumentius's report, declared that no one was more suitable for the job than Frumentius himself. Consecrated as the first Bishop of Aksum around the year 330 AD, Frumentius returned to the kingdom he now considered home. The man who had arrived as a slave now returned as the head of the national church, known to Ethiopians for all time as Abba Salama, the "Father of Peace."

This captivating tale of providence and faith finds powerful corroboration in the archaeological and numismatic record left by King Ezana himself. His early inscriptions and coins are purely pagan. A magnificent granite monument in Aksum, known as the Ezana Stone, celebrates his military victories in three languages—Ge'ez, Sabaean, and Greek—and gives thanks to the pagan gods Astar, Beher, Meder, and especially his divine ancestor, the invincible Mahrem (identified with the Greek Ares). The gold, silver, and bronze coins from the first part of his reign are similarly stamped with the pre-Christian disk-and-crescent symbol.

Then, around the mid-4th century, a dramatic change occurs. A later inscription, also celebrating a military victory, omits any mention of the old pantheon. Instead, Ezana attributes his success to the "Lord of Heaven and Earth" and speaks of his faith in the Father, the Son, and the Holy Spirit. This was a clear and public declaration of his new Christian faith. The most widespread and definitive statement of this conversion, however, was broadcast on the empire's currency. In a revolutionary act, Ezana replaced the disk-and-crescent with the Christian cross on all his coins. Aksum thus became one of the very first states in the world to feature the cross on its coinage, a powerful symbol of the new official religion that was now proclaimed on every transaction within the empire and along its far-flung trade routes.

Ezana's conversion was a moment of immense significance. Coming shortly after Emperor Constantine had legalized and begun to favor Christianity in the Roman Empire, it brought Aksum into the diplomatic and cultural orbit of the Christian Mediterranean world. The decision to seek a bishop from Alexandria forged a link with the Coptic Church of Egypt that would shape the identity of Ethiopian Christianity for the next 1,600 years. A letter from the Arian Roman Emperor Constantius II, addressed to Ezana and his brother Saizana, survives, in which the emperor unsuccessfully tries to persuade the Aksumite rulers to depose Frumentius for his orthodox Athanasian beliefs and replace him with an Arian bishop. The Aksumite kings refused, cementing their commitment to the Nicene orthodoxy that Athanasius championed.

The century and a half following Ezana's conversion saw Christianity consolidate its hold on the kingdom, but it was a faith largely confined to the royal court and the main trade routes. The deeper Christianization of the highlands was accomplished by a group of missionaries who arrived in the late 5th century, known as the Nine Saints. Tradition holds they came from various parts of the Roman Empire, including Syria, Constantinople, and Anatolia. They were likely fleeing persecution that followed the Council of Chalcedon in 451, a major church council that had caused a schism in the Christian world. The council's pronouncements on the dual nature of Christ were rejected by the churches of Alexandria and Antioch. The Nine Saints brought their non-Chalcedonian, or Miaphysite, theology to Ethiopia, which aligned with the position of the Coptic Church and became the definitive doctrine of Ethiopian Orthodoxy.

These missionary monks did more than just preach. They founded monasteries, which became centers of learning and evangelization, often built on old pagan worship sites. Figures like Abba Aregawi, who founded the famous cliff-top monastery of Debre Damo, and Abba Pantelewon, who established a monastery on the outskirts of Aksum, spread the faith far beyond the capital. Their most enduring contribution, however, was a monumental scholarly achievement: the translation of the Bible into Ge'ez. Working from Greek texts, these saints and their disciples painstakingly rendered the scriptures into the local Semitic language. This act not only made the Christian message accessible to the broader population but also sanctified the Ge'ez language, elevating it to the status of a liturgical and literary tongue. This translation included books such as the Book of Enoch and the Book of Jubilees, which were subsequently lost in their original languages but preserved for posterity only in their Ge'ez versions.

The full flowering of this new Christian identity came in the early 6th century during the reign of King Kaleb, the most celebrated of the Aksumite rulers after Ezana. Under Kaleb, Aksum reached its zenith of territorial power and international prestige, becoming a champion of Christendom on the world stage. His reign coincided with a major crisis across the Red Sea in the kingdom of Himyar in modern-day Yemen. The Himyarite king, Yusuf As'ar Yath'ar, known as Dhu Nuwas, had converted to Judaism and in about 523 AD began a brutal persecution of the Christian population in his kingdom. He attacked the Aksumite garrison at Zafar, burned its churches, and then laid siege to the Christian stronghold of Najran. After the city surrendered under a promise of amnesty, Dhu Nuwas had its Christian inhabitants massacred, an event that sent shockwaves throughout the Christian world.

Refugees from Najran reached the court of the Byzantine Emperor Justin I, who, recognizing Aksum as the preeminent Christian power in the region, urged King Kaleb to intervene. Answering the call to defend his co-religionists, Kaleb amassed a huge fleet and army. Around 525 AD, with logistical support from the Byzantines, he launched a massive invasion across the Red Sea. The Aksumite forces defeated the Himyarite army, and Dhu Nuwas was killed in the fighting. Kaleb appointed a Christian Himyarite as his viceroy and remained in Yemen for several months to restore the churches and solidify Aksumite rule. This campaign was the high-water mark of Aksumite power. King Kaleb, celebrated as a saint in the Ethiopian tradition, had projected his empire's might across the sea, defended the faith, and secured Aksum's control over the lucrative South Arabian trade routes.

This golden age was also reflected in cultural and architectural achievements. It is believed that the first great Church of Our Lady Mary of Zion was built in Aksum during this period, likely initiated in the time of Ezana and Frumentius. This church, which according to Ethiopian tradition would become the resting place of the Ark of the Covenant, established Aksum as the nation's holy city and became the traditional site for the coronation of Ethiopian emperors for centuries to come. The architectural style of this and other basilicas showed influences from Syria and the wider Byzantine world, a testament to the kingdom's deep integration with global Christianity. Underpinned by a vibrant Christian faith, a rich literary tradition in Ge'ez, and a military capable of projecting power across the sea, the Aksumite Empire in the age of Kaleb was a civilization at the peak of its confidence and influence. Yet the enormous resources expended in the Yemenite campaigns, and the challenge of maintaining a vast overseas territory, may have also sown the seeds of the empire's eventual decline.

CHAPTER FIVE: The Zagwe Dynasty and the Rock-Hewn Churches of Lalibela

The golden age of Aksum, marked by overseas conquests and a flourishing international trade, could not last forever. By the 7th century, the world that had sustained Aksum's greatness was being irrevocably transformed. The rapid expansion of Islam out of the Arabian Peninsula fundamentally reconfigured the old trade networks. As Arab fleets seized control of the Red Sea, the maritime artery that had fed Aksum's wealth was slowly constricted. The once-bustling port of Adulis fell into decline, its connections to the Byzantine world severed. Power and prosperity shifted northward to the new Islamic caliphates, leaving the Christian kingdom increasingly isolated in its highland fortress.

This external pressure was compounded by internal and environmental strains. Centuries of intensive farming in the Tigrayan heartland had likely led to soil exhaustion and deforestation, weakening the agricultural base that supported the urban centers. As its commercial wealth dwindled and its lands grew less productive, the Aksumite state began to contract. The political center of gravity of the Christian kingdom began a slow but decisive drift southward, away from the now-vulnerable northern frontier and the exhausted lands around Aksum, and deeper into the more defensible, rugged terrain of the central Ethiopian highlands. This region, known as Lasta, was the homeland of the Agaw, a Cushitic-speaking people who had long been part of the Aksumite kingdom but had maintained their own distinct language and identity.

The final centuries of Aksumite rule are shrouded in obscurity, a period often referred to as a "dark age." The historical record becomes sparse, and the narrative gives way to dramatic, semi-legendary accounts. The most formidable of these tales concerns a figure known as Gudit or Yodit, a mysterious and destructive queen who, in the mid-10th century, is said to have laid waste to the kingdom. According to tradition, this non-Christian queen, possibly of a local Agaw or Jewish faith, led a devastating rebellion, burning churches and monasteries, and hunting down the last scion of the Aksumite royal house. While the historical reality of Gudit is debated by scholars, the story powerfully reflects a time of immense crisis and upheaval that saw the collapse of the old order and the definitive end of Aksum's dominance.

It was out of the ashes of this collapse that a new power arose. The rulers who consolidated their authority in the highlands of Lasta were from the local Agaw elite. They became known as the Zagwe dynasty. The name itself is thought to mean "dynasty of the Agaw." Rather than representing a complete break with the past, the Zagwe positioned themselves as the legitimate inheritors of the Aksumite legacy. They embraced the Orthodox Christianity that had become the bedrock of highland identity, maintained the crucial ecclesiastical link with the Coptic Patriarchate in Alexandria, and continued to use the Ge'ez language for liturgical and state purposes. The Zagwe did not seek to erase Aksumite history, but to appropriate it and continue it from a new geographical and ethnic center.

The Zagwe capital was established at a town named Roha, nestled deep within the mountainous territory of Lasta. This location was far more secure and defensible than Aksum had ever been, reflecting the new, more insular reality of the Ethiopian Christian state. The economy of the Zagwe kingdom was less dependent on the fickle currents of international trade and more firmly rooted in the agricultural wealth of the highlands and the control of key internal resources. One of the most vital of these was the salt trade. Blocks of salt, or *amole*, mined from the harsh Danakil Depression, were a critical commodity, used not only for consumption but also as a primary form of currency throughout the medieval Ethiopian highlands. By controlling the routes from the lowlands to the highlands, the Zagwe kings secured a vital source of revenue.

The dynasty ruled for approximately 350 years, but its history is poorly documented, and the exact number and order of its kings remain a subject of scholarly debate. Early Zagwe rulers, such as

Mara Takla Haymanot, who is traditionally considered the dynasty's founder, consolidated their power in Lasta and established the new political order. Despite their Agaw origins, they were staunch champions of the Christian faith. They endowed churches and monasteries, and their kingdom became a sanctuary for Christians from surrounding regions that were increasingly coming under the influence of Islam. The Zagwe period was one of profound architectural and artistic innovation, driven by a deep and fervent piety.

The pinnacle of this religious and cultural expression was reached during the reign of the dynasty's most famous monarch, Gebre Mesqel Lalibela, who ruled from approximately 1181 to 1221. It is under his name that the capital, Roha, would become known to the world. King Lalibela was a ruler of extraordinary vision and piety, so revered that his name became synonymous with the monumental project that would define his reign and immortalize his dynasty. He is venerated as a saint by the Ethiopian Orthodox Tewahedo Church.

According to the *Gadle Lalibela*, a hagiography written centuries after his death, the king's destiny was foretold from birth. The story recounts that upon his birth, a dense swarm of bees surrounded him without stinging him. His mother, seeing this as an omen, named him Lalibela, meaning "the bees recognize his sovereignty" in the Agaw language. His elder brother, King Harba, grew jealous of the prophecy and attempted to poison him. While in a deathlike trance from the poison, Lalibela was transported to heaven, where he was shown a celestial city of rock-hewn churches and was commanded by God to replicate it on Earth.

Whether inspired by a divine vision or a more worldly ambition, King Lalibela embarked on one of the most remarkable architectural undertakings in human history. His goal was to construct a "New Jerusalem" in the heart of his kingdom. This was a project of immense spiritual and political significance. By the late 12th century, the original Jerusalem had been captured by the forces of Saladin, making it exceedingly difficult and dangerous for Ethiopian pilgrims to make the traditional journey to the Holy

Land. Lalibela's creation offered a substitute, a holy city in the Ethiopian highlands that would serve as a national center of pilgrimage and a symbol of the kingdom's sacred status. His capital was transformed into a symbolic representation of the Holy Land, with sites given biblical names like the River Jordan (*Yordanos*) and the Mount of Olives (*Debre Zeit*).

The genius of Lalibela's project lay not in building structures up from the ground, but in carving them down into the living rock. Using the soft, red volcanic tuff of the Lasta mountains, thousands of craftsmen, and, according to legend, a host of angels who worked by night, chiseled out a complex of eleven breathtaking churches. These were not caves dug into a cliffside; they were fully realized, three-dimensional buildings, freed from the surrounding stone, complete with roofs, windows, columns, and intricate interior decorations, all hewn from a single piece of rock. The process was a marvel of engineering and planning. Workers would first trace the outline of the church on the surface of the rock, then excavate a deep trench around the perimeter to isolate the monolithic block. Only then would the painstaking work of shaping the exterior and hollowing out the interior begin, carving downwards from the roof to the floor.

The eleven churches are clustered in two main groups, bisected by the trench representing the River Jordan. A third church, Bet Giyorgis (the House of St. George), stands slightly apart, a solitary masterpiece. It is perhaps the most iconic of all the Lalibela churches, carved in the shape of a perfect Greek cross and sunk into a deep pit, its roof flush with the surrounding ground level. The northern group of churches is dominated by Bet Medhane Alem (the House of the Redeemer of the World), the largest monolithic rock-hewn church on the planet. Built in the style of a classical basilica with five naves and surrounded by a forest of thirty-four massive rectangular columns, it is a staggering feat of subterranean architecture.

Connected to it by a tunnel is Bet Maryam (the House of St. Mary), which is believed to be the oldest of the churches and is dedicated to the Virgin Mary, who is particularly venerated in

Ethiopia. Its interior is richly decorated with beautiful frescoes depicting scenes from the life of Christ and a variety of geometric patterns. The other churches in this group, including Bet Meskel (House of the Cross) and Bet Danagel (House of the Virgins), are smaller but no less impressive. The southern group includes Bet Amanuel, a stunning example of the Aksumite architectural style rendered in rock, with its characteristic alternating layers of projecting and receding stonework, and the subterranean Bet Gebriel-Rafael (House of the Angels Gabriel and Raphael), which is entered via a long, dark tunnel.

This entire complex was designed as an integrated sacred space. The churches are interconnected by a maze of underground tunnels, passages, and sunken trenches, creating a labyrinthine journey for pilgrims moving from one holy site to the next. The journey through these dark, narrow corridors, emerging into the light-filled interior of a church, was a powerful spiritual experience. The churches of Lalibela were not mere monuments; they were, and remain to this day, living places of worship, the vibrant heart of Ethiopian Christianity.

Despite the monumental achievements of King Lalibela, the Zagwe dynasty's hold on power was not absolute. Their Agaw ethnicity, while not a barrier to their Christian faith, set them apart from the Semitic-speaking elite of Tigray and Amhara who traced their lineage back to the Aksumite kings and, through them, to the biblical King Solomon and the Queen of Sheba. A prophecy began to circulate that the kingdom would only find lasting peace when the throne was restored to this "Solomonic" line. This growing ideological challenge coalesced around a figure named Yekuno Amlak, a nobleman from the Amhara region who claimed direct descent from the last Aksumite king.

The end of Zagwe rule, however, was not the result of a bloody civil war. According to tradition, the transition was a negotiated settlement, brokered by the influential church leader, Saint Tekle Haymanot. Around the year 1270, the reigning Zagwe king, Na'akueto La'ab (Lalibela's nephew and successor), was persuaded to abdicate in favor of Yekuno Amlak. In exchange for relinquishing the imperial throne, the Zagwe rulers were granted hereditary lordship over their native Lasta, retaining a privileged position within the new political order. This peaceful transfer of power marked the end of an era and the beginning of the long-ruling Solomonic dynasty, which would govern Ethiopia for the next seven centuries.

CHAPTER SIX: The Solomonic Restoration and Imperial Expansion

The year 1270 marked a profound and decisive shift in the trajectory of Ethiopian history. The transfer of power from the Zagwe dynasty, rulers from the Agaw-speaking heartland of Lasta, to Yekuno Amlak, a nobleman from the Semitic-speaking Amhara region, was more than a mere changing of the guard. It was framed as a "restoration," a return to a divinely ordained and legitimate line of succession that had been interrupted for centuries. This new dynasty, which would rule Ethiopia for over 700 years, anchored its claim not in recent military success, but in the deep and resonant past, tracing its lineage directly back to the biblical union of King Solomon of Israel and the Queen of Sheba. This foundational myth would become the ideological bedrock of the Ethiopian state, shaping its identity, justifying its imperial ambitions, and cementing a unique relationship between crown and church.

The charter for this new era was an extraordinary national epic, the *Kebra Nagast*, or "The Glory of Kings." Though its final form was compiled in the early 14th century, it synthesized centuries of oral traditions, biblical apocrypha, and local legends into a single, compelling narrative. The *Kebra Nagast* tells the story of Makeda, the beautiful and intelligent Queen of Sheba (identified with Ethiopia), who, hearing of the legendary wisdom of King Solomon, undertakes a long journey to Jerusalem to test him with riddles. Impressed by her intellect, Solomon is equally captivated by her beauty. He tricks her into spending the night with him, and from their union, a son is conceived.

Makeda returns to her kingdom and gives birth to a boy, whom she names Bayna-Lehkem, later known as Menelik. When he comes of age, Menelik travels to Jerusalem to meet his father. Solomon welcomes him with great honor, educates him in Jewish law, and begs him to stay and rule Israel after him. But Menelik is determined to return to his mother's land. Solomon reluctantly agrees and, as a parting gift, commands the firstborn sons of his Israelite nobles and priests to accompany Menelik back to Ethiopia to establish a new kingdom modeled on his own. In a final, dramatic twist, the high priest's son, Azariah, secretly removes the Ark of the Covenant from the Temple in Jerusalem and spirits it away to Ethiopia with Menelik's entourage. According to the epic, the Ark's presence sanctified Ethiopia as God's new chosen land, the "New Zion."

This powerful story provided the Solomonic dynasty with an unimpeachable mandate. The emperors were not just secular rulers; they were the descendants of Solomon, the custodians of the sacred Ark, and the heads of a new chosen people. This belief, known as the Solomonic ideology, legitimized their rule in the eyes of the populace and the powerful Orthodox Church. It also provided a divine justification for the expansion of the Christian kingdom, casting its military campaigns as holy endeavors to bring unenlightened peoples under the rule of God's anointed king.

The first of this restored line, Yekuno Amlak (r. 1270–1285), focused on consolidating the new dynasty's power. Having secured the throne, he turned his attention to neutralizing potential rivals and establishing his authority over the vast and diverse highlands. He garnered the crucial support of the Ethiopian Orthodox Church, whose leaders had reportedly brokered the peaceful abdication of the last Zagwe king. In return for the church's endorsement, the Solomonic monarchs would become its greatest patrons and protectors, granting it vast tracts of land, or *gult*, which gave the church immense economic and political power.

Under Yekuno Amlak and his immediate successors, the political center of the empire shifted decisively south from Lasta to the Amhara and Shewa regions. Unlike their predecessors, however, the early Solomonic emperors did not establish a permanent stone capital. Instead, they ruled from a mobile royal court, a vast tent city that was constantly on the move. This peripatetic capital, or *ketema*, served a practical purpose in a large, mountainous empire with limited infrastructure. By moving through the provinces, the emperor could enforce his authority, collect taxes and tribute in person, dispense justice, and provision his enormous army off the land, preventing any single region from being depleted by the court's presence. This mobile system allowed the rulers to project power and maintain control over a mosaic of different peoples and semi-autonomous provinces.

It was during the reign of one of the dynasty's most formidable warrior-kings, Amda Seyon I (r. 1314–1344), that the empire embarked on a period of dramatic and sustained military expansion. Amda Seyon was a brilliant and ruthless military strategist who transformed the Christian highland state into a true empire that dominated the Horn of Africa. His long reign was marked by a series of relentless campaigns aimed at subjugating the cluster of wealthy Muslim sultanates that lay to the southeast, most notably Ifat and Adal. These conflicts were driven by both religious fervor and hard-nosed economic calculation. The sultanates controlled the vital trade routes that connected the Ethiopian interior with the ports of Zeila and Berbera on the Gulf of Aden, and thus held a stranglehold on the region's foreign commerce.

Amda Seyon's goal was to break this monopoly and turn these rival states into tribute-paying vassals of his Christian empire. His campaigns were meticulously planned and executed with overwhelming force. The royal chronicles, written to glorify his reign, paint a vivid picture of a devout Christian warrior, the "fighting saint," who personally led his armies into battle. In 1332, following a rebellion by the Sultan of Ifat, Haq ad-Din I, Amda Seyon launched a devastating invasion. He crushed the Ifat army, killed the sultan, sacked its major towns, and replaced the ruling dynasty with a puppet ruler. He then marched his forces through a series of neighboring Muslim states, including the powerful Hadiya and Dawaro sultanates, forcing them to submit and pay hefty annual tributes in gold, livestock, and cloth.

These conquests fundamentally altered the balance of power in the region. The Christian empire now controlled the headwaters of the lucrative trade routes, siphoning off a significant portion of their wealth. To secure his gains, Amda Seyon established a permanent military presence in the conquered territories. He created a system of garrisons staffed by soldiers from the Christian highlands and appointed royal governors to oversee the new provinces. This administrative framework integrated the new territories into the imperial state and laid the foundation for centuries of highland Christian dominance over the diverse peoples of the south and east. His reign was a clear statement that the Solomonic empire was not merely a highland kingdom but the preeminent power in the entire Horn of Africa.

The successors of Amda Seyon continued his policies of consolidation and expansion. Emperors like his son, Newaya Krestos (r. 1344–1372), spent much of their reigns putting down rebellions in the newly conquered provinces and fending off counter-attacks from the resilient Adal Sultanate. The relationship between the Christian empire and its Muslim neighbors was not one of constant warfare; there were also long periods of peace and extensive commercial interaction. However, the underlying dynamic established by Amda Seyon—that of a dominant Christian empire and subordinate, tribute-paying Muslim principalities—remained the defining feature of the political landscape for the next century.

The structure of the Solomonic state that emerged during this period was a complex feudal system. At its apex was the emperor, the *Negusa Nagast* or "King of Kings," whose authority was, in theory, absolute. Below him was a hierarchy of nobles, provincial governors, and military commanders, all bound to the crown by oaths of loyalty. The emperor granted his followers rights over land (*gult*) in exchange for military service and a share of the tribute collected from the peasantry. The church was a major landholder in its own right, functioning as a parallel and immensely wealthy institution. This intricate web of obligations and patronage held the empire together, though it was often strained by the ambitions of powerful regional lords who periodically challenged the central authority of the emperor.

This era also witnessed a great cultural and religious flowering. The monasteries, endowed with wealth and protected by the crown, became vibrant centers of learning and artistic production. Scribes meticulously copied and illuminated religious manuscripts, producing stunning works of art that blended Byzantine and local Ethiopian styles. The most famous of these illustrated manuscripts, such as the Gospels and the Lives of Saints, are a testament to the deep piety and artistic sophistication of the age. Ge'ez, the ancient liturgical language, flourished as the language of scholarship and literature, with a significant body of theological and historical work being composed during this period.

This long century of Solomonic consolidation culminated in the reign of another extraordinary ruler, Emperor Zara Yaqob (r. 1434–1468). If Amda Seyon was the great military architect of the empire, Zara Yaqob was its great religious and administrative reorganizer. He was a man of intense intellectual energy and unbending religious conviction, a reformer who sought to impose doctrinal unity and centralized control over his vast and often fractious empire. He was a scholar and an author, personally composing several important theological treatises, including the *Mats'hafe Berhan* ("The Book of Light").

Zara Yaqob's primary mission was to purify the Ethiopian Orthodox Church and stamp out all traces of heresy and pre-Christian religious practices. He fiercely enforced a rigid orthodoxy, cracking down on any deviation from official doctrine. His most significant internal struggle was against a movement known as the Stephanites, followers of a monk named Abba Estifanos who challenged the emperor's secular authority over the church and questioned the practice of prostrating before the cross and icons of Mary. Zara Yaqob saw this as a direct threat to the ideological foundation of his rule and persecuted the Stephanites brutally, executing many of their leaders. He also sought to eradicate traditional religions, which he viewed as paganism, forcing mass conversions and creating a network of spies and inquisitors to enforce religious conformity.

Alongside his religious reforms, Zara Yaqob was a relentless centralizer of political power. He recognized that the semi-independent provincial governors were a constant threat to the stability of the throne. To break their power, he undertook a radical administrative overhaul, dismissing many of the hereditary regional lords and replacing them with governors appointed directly by him. In a particularly shrewd move, he often appointed his own daughters and other female relatives to these powerful posts, binding the provinces to the crown through direct family ties. He established a more elaborate and rigid court protocol, elevating the status of the monarchy and creating a greater distance between the emperor and his subjects.

Zara Yaqob's reign also marked a significant moment of re-engagement with the wider world. Concerned by the growing power of the Mamluk Sultanate in Egypt and other Muslim states in the region, he sought to forge alliances with his Christian counterparts in Europe. In 1441, he sent a delegation of Ethiopian monks from Jerusalem to the Council of Florence in Italy. This mission created a sensation in Renaissance Europe, reintroducing the semi-mythical kingdom of "Prester John" to the European imagination and initiating a period of tentative diplomatic contact. These early overtures would eventually pave the way for a more fateful encounter with Europe in the following century. Zara Yaqob left behind an empire that was more centralized, administratively coherent, and religiously unified than ever before. Yet his rigid and often brutal methods had also created deep resentments, and the powerful forces he had sought to contain would erupt with violent consequences not long after his death.

CHAPTER SEVEN: The Ethiopian-Adal War and the Portuguese Intervention (1529–1543)

The legacy of Emperor Zara Yaqob was a centralized, militantly orthodox Christian empire. However, his methods had also sown deep divisions, and the imperial structure he had so carefully constructed was placed under immense strain by his successors. The long-standing rivalry with the Muslim sultanates to the east, which had been decisively contained by warrior-kings like Amda Seyon, was about to enter a new and far more dangerous phase. The balance of power in the Horn of Africa, seemingly settled for two centuries, was about to be violently upended by the arrival of new military technology and the emergence of a charismatic, revolutionary leader who would bring the Solomonic state to the very brink of annihilation.

The primary antagonist of the Christian empire, the Sultanate of Adal, had itself undergone a significant transformation. After centuries of being battered by its powerful highland neighbor, Adal had shifted its political center inland from the vulnerable port of Zeila to the well-fortified city of Harar. This new capital, situated on a plateau, was more defensible and better positioned to project power into the interior. The sultanate was also becoming increasingly influenced by a more radical, militant form of Islam, fueled by resentment over generations of subjugation and the payment of tribute to the Christian emperors. The stage was set for a charismatic leader to harness this energy. That leader was Ahmad ibn Ibrahim al-Ghazi.

Known to Ethiopians as Ahmad "Gurey" and to the Somalis as Axmad "Gurey"—both meaning "the Left-handed"—he was not of noble birth but rose through the ranks of the Adalite military. A man of formidable will and deep religious conviction, he saw the traditional sultans of Adal as weak and corrupt, too willing to accommodate the Christian empire. Through a combination of military prowess and political maneuvering, he overthrew the ruling Walashma dynasty and seized effective control of the sultanate. He then declared a *jihad* against the Ethiopian empire, not merely to resist its dominance or raid its frontiers, but to conquer and convert it entirely.

What made Imam Ahmad's challenge so potent was his brilliant exploitation of the shifting geopolitics of the wider world. The Ottoman Empire, the new superpower of the Muslim world, was expanding its influence down the Red Sea. From Ottoman traders and allies in Arabia, Imam Ahmad was able to acquire what the Ethiopian empire almost completely lacked: firearms. He armed a core of his troops with matchlock muskets and supplemented them with light cannons, fundamentally changing the calculus of warfare in the Horn of Africa. These new weapons, combined with his charismatic leadership and the religious fervor he inspired, transformed the Adalite army from a regional rival into an instrument of conquest.

The storm broke in 1529. Imam Ahmad led his newly equipped forces out of Harar and into the Ethiopian-controlled borderlands. The reigning emperor, Lebna Dengel, a ruler who had inherited a seemingly secure and powerful empire, initially underestimated the threat. Accustomed to the traditional warfare of cavalry charges and massed infantry, he was confident his much larger armies could crush the Adalite incursion as his ancestors had done so many times before. The first major confrontation, the Battle of Shimbra Kure, fought in March 1529, delivered a profound shock.

Though the battle was tactically indecisive and the imperial army was not destroyed, the encounter demonstrated the terrifying effectiveness of the Adalite firearms. The noise, smoke, and deadly impact of the muskets and cannons sowed confusion and fear among the Ethiopian soldiers and their horses. The traditional massed charges of the Solomonic cavalry, which had for so long been the key to their military dominance, faltered against the disciplined volleys of the Adalite musketeers. Imam Ahmad's forces were able to hold their ground, inflicting heavy casualties and proving that a new era of warfare had dawned. For the first time, the Christian empire had faced an enemy it could not simply overwhelm.

Following Shimbra Kure, Imam Ahmad refined his tactics. He avoided set-piece battles where the empire's numerical superiority could be brought to bear and instead launched a series of swift, devastating raids deep into the Ethiopian heartland. Over the next few years, his forces systematically overran the southern and eastern provinces of the empire, including Dawaro, Shewa, and Bali. The mobile royal court, the traditional center of Solomonic power, was forced to flee. The conquest was brutal and methodical. Imam Ahmad's armies targeted the symbols of the Christian state: its churches and monasteries. Centuries of accumulated wealth and priceless cultural artifacts were looted or destroyed. Ancient monasteries, including the venerable Debre Libanos, were burned to the ground, and their inhabitants were killed or forcibly converted to Islam.

The psychological impact on the Christian population was catastrophic. Their world was turned upside down. The divinely ordained Solomonic kingdom, protected by the Ark of the Covenant, was being systematically dismantled. The emperor, Lebna Dengel, was reduced to the status of a fugitive in his own kingdom. For years, he was relentlessly hunted through the remote and mountainous regions of the north, unable to rally a force capable of stopping the Adalite advance. By the mid-1530s, Imam Ahmad had conquered most of the Christian highlands, including the ancient heartlands of Amhara and Lasta. He even reached the old northern capital of Aksum, where his troops damaged the revered Church of St. Mary of Zion. Much of the Christian nobility was killed or had submitted, and a significant portion of the population had been converted to Islam, either by force or by conviction. The Solomonic state had, for all practical purposes, ceased to exist as a coherent entity.

Facing complete annihilation, the desperate Emperor Lebna Dengel made a final plea to the outside world. He dispatched a message to the one power he believed could help: the Christian kingdom of Portugal. Diplomatic contact between Ethiopia and

Europe had been sporadic but ongoing for decades, driven by the persistent European legend of "Prester John," a mythical mighty Christian king thought to reside somewhere in the East. The Portuguese, who were busy building a vast maritime empire in the Indian Ocean, were particularly interested in finding this supposed ally. They saw a potential alliance with Ethiopia as a way to outflank the Ottoman Empire and control the lucrative spice trade.

Lebna Dengel's appeal for aid finally reached the Portuguese authorities in India. The request was granted. In 1541, a small but formidable Portuguese expeditionary force landed at the port of Massawa on the Red Sea coast. It consisted of 400 musketeers, equipped with state-of-the-art European firearms and light artillery, under the command of Cristóvão da Gama, the twenty-four-year-old son of the legendary explorer Vasco da Gama. They were met by the Dowager Empress Seble Wongel, Lebna Dengel's widow, as the emperor himself had died in his mountain refuge the previous year. The Portuguese force, small as it was, represented the last hope for the shattered Christian kingdom.

Young, ambitious, and brimming with crusading zeal, Cristóvão da Gama immediately took the offensive. He led his musketeers, alongside a contingent of Ethiopian loyalists, into the highlands. Their initial campaigns were stunningly successful. Their superior European weaponry and disciplined tactics allowed them to defeat several much larger Adalite armies. At the Battle of Baçente in February 1542, da Gama's small force routed a large army, capturing a strategic mountain fortress and providing a much-needed morale boost for the Ethiopian resistance. For a moment, it seemed as if the tide was turning.

Imam Ahmad, who was campaigning in the north, recognized the grave threat posed by this new enemy. The Portuguese musketeers were a force unlike any he had faced before. He appealed to his own powerful allies, the Ottomans, for assistance. A contingent of 900 Turkish and Arab musketeers, along with a number of cannons, was dispatched from Yemen to join his army. The technological playing field was now level. Imam Ahmad marched south to confront the Portuguese head-on.

The two forces met in August 1542 near Lake Ashenge at the Battle of Wofla. Da Gama, overconfident from his earlier victories, found himself facing a vastly superior enemy force, now equally well-equipped with firearms. The Portuguese-Ethiopian army was overwhelmed. The battle was a disaster. The Portuguese were routed, and Cristóvão da Gama himself was wounded, captured, and, after refusing to convert to Islam, was personally beheaded by Imam Ahmad.

The death of da Gama and the destruction of his army was a crushing blow, but it was not the end. About 140 of the Portuguese musketeers managed to escape the carnage and retreat into the mountains. There, they rendezvoused with the young new Ethiopian emperor, Gelawdewos, Lebna Dengel's son and heir. Unlike his father, Gelawdewos proved to be a resilient and inspiring military commander. He understood that the Portuguese firearms, even wielded by a handful of survivors, were a precious asset. He spent the next few months rallying the remaining loyalist forces and integrating the Portuguese veterans into his new army.

The final, decisive confrontation of the long and brutal war came on February 21, 1543, at the Battle of Wayna Daga, near Lake Tana. Emperor Gelawdewos, at the head of a combined Ethiopian-Portuguese force, faced the main Adalite army, led by Imam Ahmad in person. The battle was hard-fought, with both sides understanding that everything was at stake. The outcome was decided not by grand strategy, but by a single shot. During the fighting, Imam Ahmad, who was leading his men from the front, was struck and killed by a bullet. According to tradition, the fatal shot was fired by a Portuguese musketeer.

The death of the Imam had an immediate and catastrophic effect on the Adalite army. Their entire cause had been built around his personal charisma and military genius. With their leader gone, their morale shattered completely. The army dissolved into a rout, pursued and cut down by the triumphant forces of Emperor Gelawdewos. The victory was total and absolute. The fourteen-year-long invasion that had brought the Christian kingdom to its knees was finally over.

The Christian empire had been saved from extinction, but the cost had been immense. The war had left both the Ethiopian highlands and the Adal Sultanate utterly devastated. Entire provinces were depopulated, cities and towns were in ruins, and a generation had been lost to warfare and famine. The political and social fabric of the region had been torn apart. While the Solomonic dynasty had survived, the empire that Emperor Gelawdewos now ruled was a shadow of the one his father had inherited. The near-total collapse had created a massive power vacuum, leaving the weakened and exhausted kingdom dangerously vulnerable to new groups who would soon begin to move into the ravaged land.

CHAPTER EIGHT: The Gondarine Period: Castles and Cultural Renaissance

The cataclysmic war against the Adal Sultanate had saved the Solomonic dynasty, but at a terrible price. The Christian empire, though victorious, was a shattered and depopulated land. The conflict had not only devastated the highlands but had also created a vast power vacuum. Into this void swept the Oromo people, a pastoralist group from the south who embarked on a massive and sustained migration, permanently altering the demographic and political map of the region. For the newly restored Emperor Gelawdewos and his immediate successors, the primary task was survival. Their reigns were a long, arduous struggle to reassert control, rebuild the shattered state, and fend off the continuing pressure of Oromo expansion.

This century of crisis exposed a fundamental weakness in the traditional structure of the Solomonic state: its mobility. For centuries, the emperors had ruled from a constantly moving royal camp, a vast tent city that served as a peripatetic capital. This system had been effective for projecting power and collecting tribute in a stable empire, but in an age of constant, multi-front warfare, it proved to be a liability. The mobile court was vulnerable, and the lack of a secure, permanent center made it difficult to establish lasting administrative control. The trauma of the war and the new reality of a kingdom under siege created a powerful impetus for a radical change. The era of the wandering court was over; the empire needed a fortress, a capital, a permanent heart.

This new chapter in Ethiopian history began in earnest with the accession of Emperor Fasilides in 1632. After decisively dealing with the last vestiges of a Catholic presence by expelling the Jesuit missionaries who had caused so much religious and political turmoil, Fasilides turned his attention to establishing a new, permanent imperial center. He chose a site on a high basaltic ridge in the fertile lands north of Lake Tana. The location, Gondar, was strategically brilliant. It was protected by surrounding mountains, blessed with a mild climate, and had a plentiful water supply from the Angereb and Qaha rivers. It was far from the vulnerable eastern and southern frontiers but well-positioned to control the major internal trade routes. In 1636, Fasilides broke with a millennium of tradition and began the construction of a permanent capital, a city that would become the political, religious, and cultural center of Ethiopia for the next two centuries.

The centerpiece of Fasilides' new city was the Fasil Ghebbi, or Royal Enclosure, a vast, fortified compound that would house the emperors and their courts. Within this seventy-thousand-square-meter walled complex, Fasilides and his successors would embark on a unique and sustained building program, creating an architectural landscape unlike anything seen in Ethiopia before. The result was a stunning collection of castles, palaces, and administrative buildings that gave the city its nickname, the "Camelot of Africa." The architectural style that emerged was a fascinating and uniquely Ethiopian synthesis. The building techniques showed the clear influence of the Portuguese military engineers who had accompanied Cristóvão da Gama, particularly in the use of stone and lime mortar and the construction of round, turreted towers. Yet, this was blended with older Ethiopian traditions, recalling the monumental stonework of Aksum, alongside possible influences from Moorish and Indian architecture, brought to the region by traders and craftsmen.

The first and most imposing of these structures was Fasilides' own castle. A massive, three-story stone edifice with a crenelated parapet and four domed towers, it projected an unmistakable image of power and permanence. It contained an enormous reception hall, dining rooms, and private quarters for the emperor. Its design set the precedent for the entire enclosure, a style of fortified residence that was both a defensible fortress and a luxurious palace. A short distance from the main compound, Fasilides also constructed a beautiful two-story bathing pavilion, set in the middle of a large, rectangular pool. This structure, known as Fasilides' Bath, was surrounded by a walled enclosure with watchtowers and was likely used for recreational and ceremonial purposes. It remains one of the most picturesque and best-preserved examples of Gondarine architecture, and to this day it is the central focus of the vibrant Timkat (Epiphany) festival, when the pool is filled with water for a mass baptismal ceremony.

Fasilides' successors continued his ambitious building program, each adding their own palaces and halls to the Royal Enclosure, creating a layered tapestry of stone. His son, Yohannes I, built a library and a chancellery, contributing to the administrative infrastructure of the new capital. It was Yohannes's son, Iyasu I, known as "Iyasu the Great," who built the most elegant and ornate of the Gondarine castles. His palace was said to have been more lavish than his grandfather's, adorned with ivory, gold leaf, and precious stones, its ceilings covered with stunning paintings. The chronicles of his reign describe a sophisticated and luxurious court life within its walls, a far cry from the austerity of a mobile military camp. Later emperors, such as Dawit III and Bakaffa, added their own structures, while the powerful Empress Mentewab, wife of Bakaffa, built a graceful, banqueting-hall-like castle of her own in the 18th century. The Fasil Ghebbi was not just a collection of residences; it was a bustling city within a city, containing churches, scriptoriums, archives, stables, and even cages for the imperial lions, symbols of the Solomonic monarchy.

The stability provided by this fixed capital fostered an extraordinary cultural renaissance. With the court and the church hierarchy now settled in one place, Gondar became a magnet for artists, scholars, musicians, and theologians. This period saw the emergence of a distinctive "Gondarine school" of painting. While still focused on religious themes, this new style broke from the more abstract, two-dimensional forms of the past. Figures became more lifelike and expressive, compositions became more complex and crowded, and the use of rich, vibrant colors became a hallmark of the school. Church walls across the country, but especially in the vicinity of Gondar, were covered with magnificent murals depicting the Holy Trinity, the life of the Virgin Mary, the exploits of the saints, and the gruesome fates of martyrs. These paintings were not just decoration; they were theological texts for a largely illiterate population, vivid visual narratives of the Christian faith.

The undisputed masterpiece of this artistic flourishing is the church of Debre Berhan Selassie (Trinity at the Mount of Light), located on a small hill just outside Gondar. Built in the late 17th century, its modest stone exterior gives little hint of the astonishing beauty within. The interior of the church is a jewel box of Gondarine art. Every square inch of the walls is covered with brightly colored murals depicting scenes from the Old and New Testaments. But it is the ceiling that is the church's crowning glory. The wooden beams are covered with the serene, wide-eyed faces of eighty angels, their gazes directed down upon the worshippers below, creating an unforgettable image of the celestial host. According to local tradition, the church was miraculously saved from destruction during a Dervish raid in the 1880s when a massive swarm of bees descended from its eaves and drove off the attackers.

Gondar also became a center of intense intellectual and theological debate. The establishment of a permanent court and a stable ecclesiastical leadership allowed for doctrinal controversies that had been simmering for centuries to come to the forefront. The Ethiopian Orthodox Church became embroiled in complex and often bitter disputes over the nature of Christ, a legacy of the early schisms of the Christian church. The main point of contention was how to articulate Christ's perfect divinity and perfect humanity in one person. One school of thought, the *Tewahdo* (Unionist), which was the traditional doctrine of the Alexandrian and Ethiopian churches, maintained that the divine and human natures were perfectly united into a single nature without separation, confusion, or alteration.

However, two rival doctrines emerged and gained powerful adherents in different regions of the country. The *Qibat* (Unction) school argued that the union of divinity and humanity was made possible through the anointing of the Holy Spirit, a position that some of its opponents claimed overemphasized Christ's humanity. Another school, the *Sost Lidet* (Three Births), held that Christ had three births: one eternal birth from the Father, one in time from the Virgin Mary, and a third through the anointing of the Holy Spirit at his baptism. Emperors like Yohannes I and Iyasu I spent a great deal of their reigns presiding over church councils, attempting to resolve these disputes and enforce a unified doctrine. These debates, while seemingly obscure, were matters of immense political importance, as different monastic orders and regional elites championed competing theologies, often as a proxy for their own political ambitions.

The great rulers of the Gondarine period were not just builders and patrons; they were active shapers of the nation's political and religious identity. Emperor Fasilides, after casting out the Jesuits, firmly re-established the traditional religious link with the Coptic Patriarchate of Alexandria, requesting a new Abuna, or head of the church, from Egypt. This act restored the ancient ecclesiastical connection that had been a cornerstone of Ethiopian identity since the 4th century. His son, Yohannes I, was a deeply pious ruler who sought to solidify the Orthodox character of the state. He is best remembered for his 1668 decree at a church council that mandated religious segregation. He ordered that Muslims, who were mostly traders and artisans, had to live in a separate quarter of Gondar, a policy also applied to the *Beta Israel*, the Ethiopian Jewish community. While this policy may have been intended to reduce religious friction, it created a lasting social stratification within the capital.

The apogee of the Gondarine era came during the reign of Iyasu I, or Iyasu the Great (1682–1706). He was an ideal monarch in the Gondarine mold: a successful military commander who led campaigns to the south and east to reassert imperial authority, a diligent administrator who reformed the empire's tax system, and a great patron of art and architecture who presided over the most brilliant period of the Gondar court. He was also a devout churchman who took his role as head of the church seriously, chairing councils and attempting to heal the doctrinal rifts that plagued it. His reign was the high-water mark of the period's power and prestige. However, his life ended in tragedy. Weary of the constant political intrigue, he abdicated and retired to a monastery on an island in Lake Tana. In his absence, his son, Tekle Haymanot, usurped the throne and, in 1706, had his father assassinated.

This act of patricide was a profound shock to the system. It shattered the aura of sacred inviolability that surrounded the monarchy and ushered in an era of instability and moral decay at the imperial court. The next few decades were characterized by a series of short, ineffective reigns, with emperors often being poisoned or overthrown by ambitious relatives and court factions. Power began to fall into the hands of those who could control the court from behind the scenes. The most successful and powerful of these figures was Empress Mentewab. As the wife of the strong but short-reigned Emperor Bakaffa, she became regent for her young son, Iyasu II, upon Bakaffa's death in 1730. She was a woman of extraordinary political skill and ambition, and she effectively ruled the empire for decades, first as regent for her son and then as the power behind the throne for her grandson, Iyoas. She was a great patron of the arts, building the magnificent Qusquam monastery and church complex on a hill overlooking Gondar.

Mentewab's long reign, however, further accelerated the decentralization of power. To buttress her position at court, she surrounded herself with her own relatives from her native province of Qwara, granting them high offices and vast estates. This created resentment among the established nobility of Gondar and other regions. The imperial army, once a unified force loyal to the emperor, was increasingly replaced by the private armies of these powerful regional lords. The emperor in Gondar, surrounded by the splendor of his castles, was slowly becoming a pawn in the power struggles of his over-mighty vassals. The golden age of Gondar was fading, and the unified state so carefully constructed by Fasilides was beginning to fracture, setting the stage for a new and chaotic era in which the emperors would reign, but they would no longer rule.

CHAPTER NINE: Zemene Mesafint: The Era of Princes and Warlords

The magnificent stone castles of Gondar, built to symbolize a new era of permanence and centralized power, soon became gilded cages for the emperors they were meant to house. The patricide of Iyasu the Great in 1706 had cracked the sacred aura of the monarchy, and the long, manipulative reign of Empress Mentewab had fatally weakened its authority. By propping up her power with her own relatives from Qwara, she had institutionalized the very factionalism the Gondarine state was built to overcome. The imperial throne, once the absolute center of the Ethiopian universe, was about to become a hollow crown, a powerless prize to be fought over by a new generation of ruthlessly ambitious regional warlords. This chaotic and bloody chapter in Ethiopian history, lasting nearly a century, is known as the *Zemene Mesafint*, the "Era of the Princes" or "Era of the Judges," a name that deliberately echoes the biblical Book of Judges, a time when "there was no king in Israel: every man did that which was right in his own eyes."

The unraveling began in earnest with the death of Empress Mentewab's son, Emperor Iyasu II, in 1755. The throne passed to his own young son, Iyoas I. The new emperor was a child, but his parentage embodied the deep fissures within the state. His father was a Solomonic king, but his mother, Welete Bersabe, was the sister of a powerful Oromo chieftain from the Yejju clan. This Oromo lineage, which Iyasu II had embraced to secure alliances, now came to the fore. The young emperor, more comfortable speaking the Oromo language than the Amharic of the court, surrounded himself with his Oromo relatives. Empress Mentewab, the formidable dowager, suddenly found her Qwaran faction being eclipsed by the emperor's Yejju kin. The court at Gondar devolved into a bitter struggle between the Qwarans and the Yejju, with the established Amhara nobility of the capital looking on with disgust and alarm.

Unable to control her grandson or his powerful Oromo relations, the aging Mentewab made a fateful decision. She sought a strongman to restore order and reassert the influence of the traditional elite. She sent for the most powerful and feared provincial ruler in the empire: Ras Mikael Sehul of Tigray. Mikael was a man of extraordinary cunning, military skill, and utter ruthlessness. He had spent decades consolidating his rule over the northern province of Tigray, crushing his rivals and building a formidable army. In 1769, he answered the Empress's call and marched on Gondar at the head of a massive army, not as a servant of the crown, but as its master.

Ras Mikael arrived in the capital and quickly made his presence felt. He was a force of nature, a seasoned warlord in his seventies who possessed an unquenchable thirst for power. He swiftly outmaneuvered the Yejju faction and established himself as the undisputed guardian of the throne. However, he soon found Emperor Iyoas I to be an ungrateful and recalcitrant puppet. When the young emperor attempted to conspire against him, Ras Mikael did the unthinkable. In May 1769, he had the Emperor Iyoas I, the anointed scion of the Solomonic line, summarily murdered. This was not a hidden assassination in a distant monastery; it was a brazen act of regicide by a vassal, shattering what little remained of the monarchy's mystique. To the horror of the court, Mikael had the emperor strangled with a strip of silk, an execution method supposedly reserved for royalty to avoid the shedding of their sacred blood.

The murder of Iyoas I is the event that traditionally marks the beginning of the Zemene Mesafint. It demonstrated that ultimate power no longer resided with the emperor in his castle, but with whichever warlord commanded the strongest army. Ras Mikael promptly installed a new emperor, a powerless elderly prince named Yohannes II, whom he plucked from a royal prison. When Yohannes II showed a spark of independence, Mikael had him poisoned within months. He then placed yet another puppet, Tekle Haymanot II, on the throne. Ras Mikael Sehul had become the ultimate kingmaker and kingbreaker, and the Solomonic throne was now his personal property.

Mikael Sehul's brutal dominance over Gondar provoked a massive backlash. The other regional lords, particularly the powerful nobles of Amhara and the Yejju Oromo, were not prepared to accept the supremacy of a Tigrayan master. A great coalition of provincial armies, including those of Gojjam and Lasta, marched on Gondar to dislodge the tyrant. In a series of three epic encounters known as the Battles of Sarbakusa in 1771, Mikael Sehul's forces were defeated. He was forced to retreat back to his Tigrayan heartland, leaving a power vacuum in the capital. The coalition that had defeated him soon fell to fighting amongst themselves, and the chaos escalated. For the next century, the Ethiopian empire would cease to exist as a unified state, fracturing into a collection of de facto independent fiefdoms.

After the initial storm of Ras Mikael's reign of terror had passed, a new, more stable pattern of political control emerged. Real power in the central highlands coalesced in the hands of the Yejju Oromo dynasty. These were the descendants of the same group that had been rivals to Empress Mentewab's faction. Having converted to Christianity and intermarried with the Amhara nobility, they established their power base in the province of Begemder and seized control of the office of *Ras-Bitwoded*, or Chief of the Nobles, effectively making them the regents of the empire. From their provincial capital at Debre Tabor, they would rule what remained of the imperial center for nearly eighty years.

The founder of this Yejju ascendancy was Ras Ali I, who rose to prominence in the 1780s. He and his successors, most notably the powerful Ras Gugsa and Ras Ali II, became the new guardians of the puppet emperors in Gondar. Their rule was a delicate balancing act. They legitimized their authority by acting in the name of the Solomonic monarch, whom they protected and controlled, but their actual power depended entirely on their military strength and their ability to forge alliances with other regional lords. The Yejju regents were never able to establish total control over the entire empire; their authority was constantly challenged by the rulers of Tigray, Gojjam, and Semien.

The political map of Ethiopia during the Zemene Mesafint was a constantly shifting mosaic of warring principalities. In the north, Tigray remained a major power center. After the death of Mikael Sehul, the province was often riven by internal conflict, but periodically a strong leader would emerge to unify it. The most notable of these was Ras Wolde Selassie, who ruled Tigray for over twenty-five years at the end of the 18th and beginning of the 19th centuries. He was a shrewd and forward-looking ruler who encouraged foreign trade through the port of Massawa and even welcomed European travelers, hoping to acquire firearms to challenge the Yejju dominance.

To the west of Tigray lay the rugged, mountainous region of Semien, whose rulers, like Dejazmach Wube Haile Maryam, commanded formidable armies and controlled the key trade routes leading to Sudan. To the south of Lake Tana, the province of Gojjam was another fiercely independent heartland of Amhara nobility, its leaders constantly maneuvering for greater power and frequently challenging the Yejju regents. The imperial city of Gondar itself became a tragic pawn in these struggles. The city was repeatedly sacked and burned by competing armies, its population brutalized, and its magnificent castles fell into disrepair, becoming little more than barracks for the troops of whichever warlord was temporarily in control.

Amid this landscape of endemic chaos and civil war, one region managed to achieve a remarkable degree of stability and independence. The province of Shewa, located on the southern edge of the Christian highlands, effectively seceded from the crumbling empire. Under a local line of Amhara rulers who also claimed Solomonic descent, Shewa sealed its mountain passes and turned its back on the incessant conflicts of the north. Rulers like Asfa Wossen and Wossen Seged established a hereditary monarchy, created an effective administration, and built a loyal army. While the warlords of the north were exhausting themselves in pointless internecine warfare, the rulers of Shewa were expanding their kingdom southward, incorporating new territories and peoples, and building a prosperous and well-organized state. This isolation would prove to be a crucial advantage, allowing

Shewa to husband its resources and emerge as a major power in the latter half of the 19th century.

The incessant warfare of the Zemene Mesafint had a devastating impact on Ethiopian society. The large, personal armies of the various *mesafint* crisscrossed the land, living off the labor of the peasantry. Soldiers pillaged farms, burned villages, and stole livestock, leaving a trail of destruction and famine in their wake. Trade was disrupted, and the general security that is essential for agricultural prosperity vanished. For the common farmer, life was precarious and brutal, subject to the whims of the nearest powerful man. The social contract between ruler and ruled had completely broken down.

Religion, which had once been the great unifier of the Christian kingdom, became just another weapon in the political arsenal of the warlords. The complex theological disputes that had animated the Gondarine court were now used to create ideological divisions and rally support. The Gojjami lords, for instance, became champions of the *Qibat* (Unctionist) doctrine, which emphasized Christ's humanity. The Yejju and their allies in Begemder often favored the *Sost Lidet* (Three Births) doctrine. Meanwhile, the monastic houses of Tigray and the traditionalist center of Debre Libanos in Shewa remained bastions of the established *Tewahdo* (Unionist) faith. Warlords would call church councils to excommunicate their rivals on doctrinal grounds, and battles were often fought under the banner of competing interpretations of the nature of Christ. The church, like the state, was deeply fractured and politicized.

By the 1840s, the Zemene Mesafint had entered its final and most chaotic phase. The Yejju regency was now in the hands of Ras Ali II, a man who, despite his title, struggled to exert the same authority as his predecessors. His mother, the Empress Menen Liben Amede, a shrewd and politically ambitious woman, held much of the real power. Ras Ali II's rule was contested by a host of powerful rivals. The most formidable of these was Dejazmach Wube Haile Maryam of Semien and Tigray, who had ambitions of reuniting the empire under his own rule. Another major player was the powerful and respected Dejazmach Goshu Zewde of Gojjam. The great lords of the era met in a series of bloody battles, such as the Battle of Debre Tabor in 1842, where Ras Ali II, with the help of Dejazmach Wube, managed to defeat a coalition led by Dejazmach Goshu. But these victories were never decisive; they merely rearranged the pieces on a chessboard of perpetual conflict.

The country was exhausted. A century of disunity and civil war had impoverished the land and sapped the morale of its people. The glorious legacy of Aksum, Lalibela, and Gondar seemed a distant memory. The idea of a unified Christian Ethiopia, ruled by a single, powerful Solomonic emperor, had become little more than a theoretical concept, a prayer recited in the liturgy of a divided church. The constant state of war had created a deep yearning for peace, order, and a leader strong enough to impose his will on the quarreling princes.

That leader was about to emerge from the most unlikely of places. In the remote western borderland province of Qwara, the very region that Empress Mentewab had come from, a minor nobleman named Kassa Hailu was beginning to make a name for himself. Born into the chaos of the Zemene Mesafint and orphaned at a young age, Kassa had been educated in a monastery but had chosen the life of a soldier. After his local governorship was taken from him, he refused to submit and instead took to the hills, becoming a *shifta*—a bandit or outlaw. But Kassa was no ordinary bandit. He was a brilliant guerrilla tactician, a man of immense personal charisma, and he possessed a burning, messianic vision of a reunited, reformed, and modern Ethiopia. He gathered a band of loyal followers and began to challenge the local representatives of Ras Ali II. His small victories soon grew into larger ones, and his reputation spread like wildfire. The warlords of the Zemene Mesafint, secure in their provincial power, were about to be confronted by a revolutionary force they could neither understand nor contain. The age of princes was drawing to a close, and the age of a unifier was about to begin.

CHAPTER TEN: The Rise of a Unifier: Emperor Tewodros II

The century of chaos known as the Zemene Mesafint had bled Ethiopia white. The great provincial lords, in their endless struggle for supremacy, had ravaged the land, impoverished the peasantry, and reduced the Solomonic throne to a powerless trinket. The national spirit, once the bedrock of the empire, had fractured along the lines of regional ambition and theological dispute. By the middle of the 19th century, the country was a patchwork of warring fiefdoms, a ghost of its former glory. There was a deep yearning in the air for an end to the bloodshed, a messianic hope for a prophesied leader who would crush the warlords, restore the unity of the empire, and usher in an age of justice and peace. That hope would find its incarnation in a man of ferocious ambition and revolutionary vision, a man who began his career as a common outlaw: Kassa Hailu of Qwara.

Kassa was a product of the very chaos he would later seek to destroy. Born around 1818 in the remote western province of Qwara, his lineage was noble but minor, his connection to the Solomonic line tenuous at best. His father, a local governor, died when Kassa was young, and his family was cast into poverty. Like many bright young men of his time with few prospects, he was sent to a monastery for his education, where he learned to read and write and became deeply versed in the scriptures. But the contemplative life was not for him. The world outside the monastery walls was one of war and opportunity, and Kassa chose the path of the soldier. After a brief and frustrating stint as a minor official, his district was taken from him by the machinations of Empress Menen, the mother of the Yejju regent, Ras Ali II. Rather than submit to a system he viewed as corrupt, Kassa took to the hills. He became a *shifta*.

In the context of the Zemene Mesafint, a *shifta* was more than a mere bandit. While Kassa and his followers certainly engaged in plunder to survive, they often operated under a code of conduct that appealed to the downtrodden peasantry. He cultivated a reputation as a Robin Hood figure, a champion of the common man against the rapacious and disorganized armies of the regional lords. He was a natural leader of men, possessed of a magnetic charisma, boundless physical courage, and a genius for guerrilla warfare. His band of outlaws grew into a disciplined and fanatically loyal army. He understood that to win, he needed the support of the people, and he earned it by protecting them from the depredations of other armies and by promising a future free from the endless cycle of war and exploitation. His small corner of the country became a haven of relative order, a microcosm of the unified state he dreamed of building.

His growing power could not be ignored by the great warlords. Empress Menen, hoping to co-opt the troublesome *shifta*, arranged for him to marry her granddaughter, Tewabech Ali. For a time, Kassa served his new father-in-law, Ras Ali II, but the alliance was an uneasy one. Kassa was too ambitious to remain a subordinate, and the decadent, faction-ridden court of the Yejju regent at Debre Tabor filled him with contempt. In 1852, he broke away and resumed his rebellion, this time not as a mere outlaw, but as a contender for supreme power. The established princes of Ethiopia were about to discover that the man they had dismissed as a minor nuisance was, in fact, their destroyer.

Kassa's path to the imperial throne was a lightning campaign of astonishing speed and audacity. He moved with a decisiveness that consistently caught his larger, more ponderous rival armies off guard. His first major target was the powerful and respected Dejazmach Goshu Zewde of Gojjam. At the Battle of Gur Amba in November 1852, Kassa's smaller but better-disciplined force completely crushed Goshu's army. The victory was total; Goshu himself was killed in the fighting. The conquest of Gojjam sent a shockwave through the ranks of the nobility. Kassa was no longer just a successful rebel; he was a kingmaker in his own right.

Next, he turned his attention to the heart of the Zemene Mesafint's power structure: the Yejju dynasty. Ras Ali II, finally roused to the magnitude of the threat, gathered a massive army, the last great host of the Yejju era. The two forces met on June 29, 1853, at the Battle of Ayshal. It was the final, decisive confrontation that brought the Era of the Princes to a bloody conclusion. Kassa's strategic brilliance and the superior morale of his troops carried the day. The Yejju army was annihilated, its commanders killed or captured. Ras Ali II fled the battlefield in disgrace and disappeared from history, seeking refuge in his ancestral lands. With this single victory, Kassa had shattered the political order that had dominated central Ethiopia for nearly a century.

Only one major rival remained: Dejazmach Wube Haile Maryam of Semien and Tigray. Wube was the most powerful lord in the north and harbored his own ambitions of becoming emperor. He had control of the Abuna, the head of the church, and saw himself as the last defender of the old order against the upstart from Qwara. Gathering his forces, Wube marched south to confront Kassa. The final battle for control of the empire took place at Derasge on February 9, 1855. Once again, Kassa's superior generalship proved decisive. Dejazmach Wube was defeated and taken prisoner. In less than three years, Kassa Hailu, the former *shifta*, had defeated, one by one, all the great warlords of the land. The Zemene Mesafint was over.

Two days after his final victory, in the church at Derasge, Kassa Hailu was anointed and crowned by Abuna Salama III as Emperor of Ethiopia. He cast aside his birth name and took the throne name Tewodros II. The choice was a masterstroke of political and religious propaganda. An ancient and widely known prophecy, the *Fekkare Iyasus* ("The Explication of Jesus"), foretold the coming of a righteous king named Tewodros who would restore the glory of the empire, destroy Islam, recapture Jerusalem, and reign for a thousand years in an era of perfect peace and prosperity. By taking this name, Kassa was declaring that he was the man of the prophecy, the divinely chosen savior of a ravaged nation. His coronation was not just a political act; it was the dawn of a new, messianic age.

Emperor Tewodros II had a revolutionary vision for the nation he now commanded. His goal was not simply to become the most powerful of the warlords, but to utterly destroy the feudal system that had produced them. He envisioned a modern, centralized state, united under the absolute authority of the emperor. His reform agenda was breathtakingly ambitious. He declared an end to the hereditary provincial governorships that had been the basis of the warlords' power. Henceforth, governors would be salaried officials appointed by and loyal only to him. He sought to create a modern, disciplined national army, paid directly by the state. This would eliminate the traditional feudal levies and, crucially, end the practice of soldiers living off the peasantry, a system known as *qurt*, which had been the scourge of the common people.

His reforms extended to every aspect of the state. He attempted to establish a unified legal code, reform the tax system to make it more equitable, and build a national network of roads to improve communication and facilitate the movement of his army. In a radical move for the time, he declared a ban on the slave trade, a practice deeply embedded in the economy of southern Ethiopia. He saw his mission as nothing less than the complete transformation of Ethiopia from a medieval relic into a modern nation capable of standing on its own in a world increasingly dominated by outside powers.

This radical agenda immediately collided with the deeply entrenched interests of the old elite. The regional nobility, though defeated on the battlefield, were not eliminated. They chafed under the rule of a man they considered a low-born usurper and rose in constant rebellion, seeking to reclaim their hereditary privileges. The highlands of Gojjam, Lasta, Tigray, and Shewa, which Tewodros had conquered with such speed, refused to be tamed. The emperor spent the majority of his reign marching his new national army from one end of the country to the other, brutally suppressing one rebellion after another. In Shewa, he captured the young heir to the local throne, a boy named Menelik, and brought him to his mountain fortress at Magdala, where he was raised and educated as a royal hostage.

Tewodros's most formidable opponent, however, was not the nobility, but the Ethiopian Orthodox Church. The church was an immensely powerful and wealthy institution, owning vast tracts of land, estimated by some to be as much as a third of the entire country. To fund his new salaried army and administration, Tewodros needed revenue, and he saw the church's "excess" wealth as the logical source. He proposed a radical plan to confiscate most church lands, leaving each parish with only enough to support a small, specified number of clergy. The thousands of priests and monks who would be dispossessed by this reform were to be conscripted into his army or become tax-paying farmers. The church reacted with fury. They saw the emperor's plan as a sacrilegious attack on the foundation of the Christian faith. The clergy, who held immense influence over the peasantry, began to preach against the emperor, denouncing him as a heretic and an enemy of God. Tewodros, the prophesied savior, soon found himself excommunicated by the very institution he sought to purify and subordinate to his new state.

The emperor's personality was as complex and volatile as his reign. He could be a man of great charm, intelligence, and compassion. He was known to dispense justice personally, and he genuinely believed his reforms were for the good of the common people. But he was also a man of terrifying rages, possessed of a deep-seated paranoia that was only exacerbated by the constant betrayals and rebellions that beset him. He had no patience for opposition, and as his plans were frustrated, his methods became increasingly brutal. He used mass executions, torture, and the taking of hostages to enforce his will. His violent temper and ruthless cruelty alienated many who had initially supported his vision of a united Ethiopia. The unifier was becoming a tyrant.

Despite his internal struggles, Tewodros was keenly aware of the world beyond his mountain kingdom. He was fascinated by European technology and saw the Christian nations of Europe as potential allies against the Ottoman Empire and its Egyptian vassals, who were pressing on his western and northern borders. He actively sought to acquire modern firearms and the expertise to manufacture them. He welcomed European missionaries, artisans, and adventurers to his court, hoping to use their skills to modernize his army and country. He established a workshop at

Gafat, near his capital at Debre Tabor, where his European craftsmen were put to work building cannons and mortars.

His most important diplomatic overture was to Great Britain. He held a deep admiration for the power and technical prowess of the British Empire and saw a fellow Christian monarch, Queen Victoria, as his natural ally. He cultivated a close friendship with the British consul, Walter Plowden, and after Plowden was killed by rebels in 1860, Tewodros personally avenged his death by slaughtering the killers. He wrote letters to Queen Victoria, proposing a joint Christian alliance against their common Muslim enemies and requesting that she send him skilled technicians. He saw himself and the Queen as equals, two Christian sovereigns with a shared purpose. It was a perception that the British government, with its imperial mindset, did not share.

By the early 1860s, the great dream of Tewodros II was beginning to crumble. His grand vision of a unified, modern state was being consumed by the fires of rebellion and the intransigence of the old order. The national army he had created was bogged down in a ceaseless campaign of internal repression, and the treasury was empty. The church had turned against him, and the nobility was in a state of permanent revolt. His rule, which had once extended over the entire empire, was shrinking, his authority recognized only in the areas where his army was physically present. He was forced to abandon his capital at Debre Tabor and retreat to the impregnable mountain fortress of Magdala, which became his last capital, his treasury, and his prison. The great unifier, the messianic figure who had promised a new age of peace and prosperity, was now an isolated and increasingly desperate ruler, besieged in his own kingdom, his great vision for Ethiopia lying in ruins around him.

CHAPTER ELEVEN: The Reign of Yohannes IV: Defending the Faith and the Nation

The suicidal act of defiance by Emperor Tewodros II at Magdala in 1868 did not bequeath a unified empire to his successor. It left a power vacuum. The victorious British expeditionary force, having accomplished its narrow objective of freeing the European hostages, had no interest in governing the country. They packed up their elephants, auctioned their surplus supplies, and marched back to the coast, leaving Ethiopia to its own devices. The country immediately reverted to the familiar and destructive politics of the Zemene Mesafint. The brief, violent dream of a centralized state had died with Tewodros, and the great regional lords, who had been cowed but not eliminated, re-emerged to stake their claim on the imperial throne.

Three main contenders dominated the landscape. In the central highlands of Lasta, Wagshum Gobeze, a powerful ruler with a strong claim to the Solomonic line, moved quickly to have himself crowned as Emperor Tekle Giyorgis II. In the south, Menelik, the young and ambitious king of Shewa who had escaped Tewodros's fortress at Magdala years earlier, consolidated his power and watched the events in the north with a calculated patience. The third and ultimately most decisive player was in the northern province of Tigray. Dejazmach Kassa Mercha, another nobleman of Solomonic descent, had played a clever game during the British invasion. While other leaders had remained aloof, Kassa had actively cooperated with the British commander, Sir Robert Napier, providing supplies and securing the route for his army. He had earned Napier's gratitude, and when the British departed, they rewarded him handsomely. Kassa was able to purchase a significant cache of modern surplus weaponry, including several artillery pieces and thousands of Snyder rifles, giving his provincial army a technological edge no other warlord in Ethiopia could match.

The newly crowned Emperor Tekle Giyorgis II, ruling from the old heartlands, could not tolerate the open defiance of his Tigrayan vassal. He demanded that Kassa Mercha pay homage and submit to his authority. Kassa refused. In 1871, Tekle Giyorgis II amassed a vast, traditional army, estimated at sixty thousand men, and marched into Tigray to crush the rebellion. Kassa Mercha's forces numbered only around twelve thousand, but they were disciplined, well-trained, and armed with the best weapons in the country. The two armies met near Adwa in July 1871 at the Battle of Assam. The result was a stunning demonstration of the new realities of warfare. Tekle Giyorgis's massive, charging host was met with withering, disciplined rifle fire and artillery bombardment. His army was routed, and the emperor himself was wounded and captured. His brief reign was over.

With his last great rival defeated, Kassa Mercha was the undisputed master of northern Ethiopia. In January 1872, he marched to the ancient, holy city of Aksum, the traditional coronation site of the greatest emperors of the past. There, he was anointed by the Abuna and crowned *Negusa Nagast* of Ethiopia, taking the throne name Yohannes IV. By choosing Aksum over Gondar, he was deliberately bypassing the decadent and faction-ridden legacy of the recent past and linking his own reign directly to the empire's ancient glory and its deep Christian foundations.

Yohannes's vision for Ethiopia was fundamentally different from the revolutionary centralism of his predecessor, Tewodros. Where Tewodros had sought to destroy the regional nobility and create a modern, salaried administration, Yohannes, himself a product of the provincial elite, sought to build a more traditional, hierarchical state. His model was not a unitary nation but a feudal confederation, a pyramid of power with himself at the very apex as the King of Kings. The great regional lords would be allowed to rule their own lands as his vassals, holding the title of *Negus*, or king, as long as they acknowledged his supreme authority, paid tribute, and provided military support when called upon. It was a more pragmatic and traditional approach, one that recognized the deeply entrenched power of the regional dynasties.

The greatest challenge to this vision was Menelik of Shewa. For the first several years of Yohannes's reign, Menelik refused to acknowledge him as emperor, styling himself as an independent king and continuing his own southward expansion. Yohannes, patient but firm, slowly tightened the screws. He consolidated his control over the central provinces of Gojjam and Wollo, effectively encircling Shewa. In 1878, faced with the prospect of a full-scale invasion by Yohannes's superior army, Menelik chose diplomacy over war. The two rulers met and negotiated the Liche Agreement. Menelik agreed to renounce his imperial ambitions and recognize Yohannes as his overlord. In return, Yohannes recognized Menelik as the hereditary *Negus* of Shewa and, in a move of profound foresight, designated him as his heir to the imperial throne. The agreement was a masterstroke of statecraft, uniting the two most powerful men in the empire and bringing Shewa back into the imperial fold without a costly civil war. Yohannes applied the same model to Gojjam, anointing his loyal general Ras Adal as *Negus* Tekle Haymanot of Gojjam and Kaffa.

For Yohannes, political unity was inseparable from religious unity. He was a man of profound and austere personal piety, a monarch who saw himself first and foremost as a defender of the Orthodox Christian faith. He believed that the chaos of the Zemene Mesafint had been caused not just by political fragmentation but also by doctrinal disunity within the church. For over a century, the Ethiopian Orthodox Church had been plagued by bitter theological disputes over the nature of Christ, with rival schools of thought like the *Sost Lidet* and *Qibat* doctrines being championed by different regional factions. Yohannes was determined to end these divisions and enforce a single, unified state religion.

In 1878, he convened a great church synod at Boru Meda, in the province of Wollo. With all the leading clergy and nobility present, he presided over the council and declared that the traditional *Tewahdo* (Unionist) doctrine was the one and only true faith of the Ethiopian empire. All other interpretations were outlawed. The Council of Boru Meda was a watershed moment, ending centuries of theological debate by imperial decree. Following the council, Yohannes issued a proclamation giving all non-Christians within his empire a stark choice: convert to Orthodox Christianity or face severe consequences, including the confiscation of their land and property. This policy was applied with particular force in the recently subjugated region of Wollo, a major center of Ethiopian Islam. Thousands of Oromo and Afar Muslims were forcibly baptized, and their leaders were given high Christian offices. While this policy forged a stronger ideological bond among the Christian elite of the highlands, it also created a legacy of deep and lasting resentment among the Muslim communities and other religious minorities.

Yohannes's obsession with defending the faith was not directed solely at internal matters. The greatest challenges of his reign came not from rebellious vassals, but from a series of external invasions that threatened the very existence of his empire. The first and most serious of these threats came from the north. The ambitious Khedive Isma'il Pasha of Egypt harbored a grand vision of an African empire that controlled the entire Nile River basin, from the Mediterranean to its source. As part of this plan, he began an aggressive expansion into the Horn of Africa from his coastal possession at Massawa. Egyptian forces pushed inland, occupying the Bogos region and its main town of Keren, territory that Yohannes considered historically part of Ethiopia. After Yohannes's diplomatic protests were ignored, the Khedive decided to end the Ethiopian problem once and for all with a full-scale invasion.

In November 1875, a well-equipped Egyptian army, led by a Danish commander, Colonel Arendrup, marched into Tigray. They were confident that their modern Remington rifles and Krupp artillery would make short work of the Ethiopian forces. Yohannes, a brilliant military strategist, drew the Egyptians deep into the mountains. At Gundet, on the banks of the Mareb River, the Ethiopian army, which had been concealed in the surrounding hills, fell upon the strung-out Egyptian column. The result was not a battle, but an annihilation. The Egyptian force was almost entirely wiped out, and their commander was killed. A vast quantity of modern weaponry fell into Ethiopian hands.

Humiliated and enraged, Khedive Isma'il dispatched a second, much larger expeditionary force the following year. This army, numbering some fifteen thousand men and led by Ratib Pasha and the American Confederate general William Loring, was one of the most powerful ever seen in the region. Yohannes responded by declaring a holy war and mobilizing the entire strength of his empire. In March 1876, the two armies met near the plain of Gura. Over two days of fierce fighting, the Ethiopian army, personally commanded by the emperor, decisively crushed the Egyptian invasion force. The victory at Gura was even more complete than the one at Gundet. It was a national triumph that secured Ethiopia's sovereignty, crippled Egypt's imperial ambitions, and earned Yohannes international respect as a formidable military leader.

No sooner had the Egyptian threat receded than a new danger emerged from the west. In the early 1880s, a charismatic religious leader in Sudan, Muhammad Ahmad, declared himself the *Mahdi*, the prophesied redeemer of Islam. His followers, known as the Mahdists or Dervishes, launched a spectacularly successful jihad that overthrew the Turco-Egyptian administration in Sudan and established a new, militant Islamic state. The Mahdists saw Emperor Yohannes, the powerful Christian ruler on their border, as a natural enemy. Their rise would soon draw Ethiopia into a new and brutal conflict.

This conflict was precipitated by the intervention of a third foreign power: Great Britain. After the Mahdists had besieged a number of Egyptian garrisons in eastern Sudan, the British, who had occupied Egypt in 1882, found themselves in a difficult position. They turned to Yohannes for help. In 1884, Yohannes signed the Hewett Treaty with Britain and Egypt. Under the terms of the treaty, Yohannes agreed to allow the besieged Egyptian soldiers to evacuate through his territory. In return, the British guaranteed that Ethiopia would regain control of the Bogos region and would have "free transit through Massawa to and from the sea for all goods, including arms and ammunition." Yohannes faithfully upheld his end of the bargain, sending his great general Ras Alula to relieve the garrisons and fight off the pursuing Mahdist forces.

The British, however, betrayed him. Just as Ethiopia was poised to regain its traditional sea access at Massawa, Great Britain actively encouraged another European power, Italy, to occupy the port in 1885. The British saw a friendly Italian presence as a useful counterbalance to French ambitions in the Red Sea. For Yohannes, this was a catastrophic breach of faith. Not only was he denied his promised access to the sea, but he now had a new, ambitious European colonial power planting its flag on his northern frontier. The Italians quickly began to push inland from Massawa, occupying villages and encroaching on territory controlled by Ras Alula. In January 1887, Alula responded. At Dogali, his forces ambushed and destroyed an Italian battalion sent to reinforce their forward positions. The battle was a major victory, temporarily halting the Italian advance, but it created a state of war between Ethiopia and Italy.

The Mahdists in Sudan, meanwhile, were enraged by Yohannes's cooperation with the European Christians and the Egyptians. They declared their own jihad against Ethiopia, launching a series of devastating raids into the western provinces. In 1888, a large Mahdist army led by Abu Anja penetrated deep into the country and sacked the old imperial capital of Gondar, burning its famous churches and carrying off thousands of its inhabitants as slaves. By early 1889, Emperor Yohannes was in an impossible position, trapped in a two-front war. In the north, the Italians were consolidating their positions, while in the west, the Mahdists were posing an existential threat to the Christian highlands.

Yohannes decided that the Mahdists were the more immediate and dangerous foe. He viewed the conflict not as a mere border war, but as a defense of Christendom itself. He gathered the grand army of the empire, a force said to number over one hundred thousand men, and marched west to the Sudanese border to confront the enemy at their stronghold of Gallabat, known to Ethiopians as Metemma. On March 9, 1889, the Ethiopian army launched a massive assault on the Mahdist fortress. The fighting was furious, but the sheer weight of the Ethiopian numbers began to tell. By the end of the day, the Mahdist defenses had been breached, and victory was in sight.

Yohannes, as was the custom for Ethiopian emperors, led his troops from the front lines, personally directing the battle and inspiring his men. It was a tradition that had served him well at Gura, but at Metemma, it would prove fatal. As the battle raged, he was struck in the chest and arm by a sniper's bullet. He was carried back to his tent, mortally wounded. He lived long enough to hear of the victory his army was winning and to name his son, Mengesha, as his heir. News of the emperor's mortal wound, however, spread like wildfire through the Ethiopian ranks. Their morale, which had been soaring in the moment of triumph, instantly collapsed. The army, leaderless and in shock, disintegrated. The great victory turned into a disastrous rout. The Mahdists, snatching victory from the jaws of defeat, pursued the retreating Ethiopians and captured the emperor's camp. They took Yohannes's body, beheaded it, and sent his head back to their capital at Omdurman as a trophy. The reign of the great warrior-emperor, the defender of the faith, had come to a sudden and tragic end on a foreign battlefield.

CHAPTER TWELVE: Emperor Menelik II and the Scramble for Africa

The news from Metemma in March 1889 sent a tremor of shock and confusion across the highlands. Emperor Yohannes IV, the great defender of the faith, was dead, killed on a foreign battlefield at the very moment of victory. His army, its leader and its spirit gone, had disintegrated. His designated heir, his son Ras Mengesha, was left with a scattered force and a weakened claim. The tragic death of the emperor did not create a unified Ethiopia mourning its fallen leader; it created a power vacuum. The carefully constructed hierarchy of vassal kings and lords that Yohannes had built was instantly dissolved, and the specter of the Zemene Mesafint, the chaotic Era of Princes, threatened to return.

Far to the south, in the well-organized and prosperous kingdom of Shewa, the news was received not with dismay, but with a sense of grim opportunity. For over a decade, *Negus* Menelik of Shewa had been a patient and powerful vassal, outwardly loyal to Yohannes but privately building his own empire-within-an-empire. While Yohannes had exhausted his resources fighting Egyptians, Mahdists, and Italians, Menelik had spent those years undertaking a relentless and highly profitable expansion to the south and east. His army was battle-hardened, loyal, and, crucially, intact. Upon hearing of Yohannes's death, Menelik did not hesitate. On the 25th of March 1889, he immediately proclaimed himself Emperor. He argued that his claim to the Solomonic throne, through a direct and uninterrupted male lineage, was at least as legitimate as that of the Tigrayan line. On November 3rd, he was formally crowned *Negusa Nagast* Menelik II. The patient king of Shewa had finally seized the imperial prize.

Menelik ascended to a throne that was far from secure. He faced the immediate challenge of his northern rival, Ras Mengesha, and the broader problem of asserting his authority over a country accustomed to regional autonomy. More pressingly, he had to contend with the growing presence of a new and ambitious

European power. The Italians, having established a colony on the Red Sea coast which they officially named Eritrea in 1890, were hungry for more. In the complex chess game of Ethiopian politics, Menelik had previously seen the Italians as a useful source of weapons and a potential ally against his overlord, Emperor Yohannes. Now, as emperor himself, he sought to formalize this relationship to secure his own position. He needed Italian arms and recognition, and the Italians believed they had found in Menelik a pliable African ruler through whom they could realize their colonial ambitions.

This convergence of interests led, on May 2, 1889, to the signing of the Treaty of Wuchale, a pact of friendship and commerce negotiated between Menelik and the Italian representative, Count Pietro Antonelli. The treaty, signed in the town of Wuchale in Wollo province, was a complex document with twenty articles covering borders, trade, and diplomatic relations. Menelik agreed to recognize Italy's new colony of Eritrea, effectively ceding the northern highlands of Hamasen and other districts. In return, Italy recognized Menelik as the Emperor of Ethiopia and promised financial and military aid. The treaty appeared, on the surface, to be a mutually beneficial agreement. But hidden within its text was a single, explosive article that would lead directly to war. This was the infamous Article 17.

The problem with Article 17 lay in its translation. The treaty was written in both Amharic and Italian, and both versions were supposed to be identical. The Amharic version of the article stated that the Emperor of Ethiopia *could* use the good offices of the Italian government to conduct his foreign affairs with other European powers. The Italian version, however, stated that the Emperor *consented to* use the Italian government for all foreign business. The difference was enormous. The Amharic text offered an optional diplomatic convenience; the Italian text imposed a mandatory obligation, effectively turning Ethiopia into an Italian protectorate. Whether this discrepancy was a deliberate deception by the Italian translator or a colossal misunderstanding remains a subject of debate, but its effect was clear. In October 1889, the Italian government, brandishing its version of the treaty, formally notified the other European powers that Ethiopia was now under its protection. The Scramble for Africa, it seemed, had claimed its final independent prize.

Menelik, busy consolidating his rule and initially focused on the benefits of the treaty, was not immediately aware of the diplomatic trap that had been sprung. It was only when he began receiving replies to his own accession announcements from heads of state like Queen Victoria, who politely informed him that they could not correspond with him directly and must now go through Rome, that the full extent of the duplicity became clear. The emperor was enraged. His wife, the formidable and deeply anti-European Empress Taytu Betul, was even more incensed, viewing the treaty as a profound insult to national honor. She became a leading voice in the court for a hardline stance against Italian encroachment. Menelik had sought an alliance of equals; he had been treated as a colonial subject.

While this diplomatic storm was brewing in the north, Menelik was aggressively pursuing the grand project that had defined his career as King of Shewa: the creation of a vast southern empire. This period of expansion, sometimes referred to as the *Agar Maqnat* or "cultivation of land," was a decades-long military endeavor that fundamentally reshaped the Horn of Africa and created the borders of modern Ethiopia. It was a process that mirrored the European colonial conquests happening elsewhere on the continent, and it was often just as brutal. Armed with an ever-increasing supply of modern European firearms, Menelik's armies marched south, east, and west, subjugating a vast array of peoples and kingdoms that had never been part of the historic highland Christian state.

The campaigns were led by a cadre of brilliant and ruthless generals. Figures like Ras Gobena Dache, himself an Oromo, played a key role in incorporating other Oromo territories into the Shewan sphere. Ras Welde Giyorgis Aboye and Dejazmach Habte Giyorgis Dinagde, who would become Minister of War, pushed the boundaries of the empire deep into the south. The conquest began in earnest in the 1870s and continued throughout Menelik's reign. The historic walled city of Harar, the last remnant of the Adal Sultanate, was conquered in 1887. The kingdoms of the Gurage, Kaffa, and the Omotic-speaking Wolayta were all brought to heel. The campaigns against the Arsi Oromo and the Kingdom of Wolayta in the 1890s were particularly bloody, resulting in massive casualties as rifle-wielding imperial soldiers faced warriors armed with spears.

This expansion was driven by a combination of motives. There was the traditional ambition of a Solomonic ruler to expand his domain, but there was also a keen awareness of the new geopolitical reality of the Scramble for Africa. Menelik knew that if he did not claim these territories, the British, French, or Italians would. In a famous circular letter sent to the European powers in 1891, he laid out his territorial claims, framing them as the "re-establishment of the ancient frontiers" of Ethiopia and boldly stating, "If powers at a distance come forward to partition Africa between them, I do not intend to be an indifferent spectator." His conquests were a preemptive Ethiopian scramble for Africa, a race to create a strategic buffer zone rich in resources like ivory, coffee, gold, and slaves.

The newly conquered territories were integrated into the empire through a system that institutionalized northern dominance. Menelik established a series of garrison towns, or *ketemas*, throughout the south, which became centers of military, political, and economic control. The lands of the conquered peoples were often confiscated and distributed to the emperor's soldiers and officials from the north, who became known as *neftenya*, or riflemen. The local populations were reduced to the status of *gabbar*, or tribute-payers, obligated to provide labor and a significant portion of their produce to their new landlords. This *neftenya-gabbar* system, while effective in securing control, created a legacy of social and economic inequality and deep-seated resentment that would persist for generations.

As he was building his empire, Menelik was also building a new capital. For centuries, the Ethiopian court had been mobile. Menelik's own capital as King of Shewa was a military camp on the chilly heights of Mount Entoto. In 1886, while Menelik was away on campaign, his wife, Empress Taytu, was drawn to the hot springs in a valley below the mountain. She decided to build a house there, and in 1887, she established a permanent base which she named Addis Ababa, or "New Flower." Menelik soon moved the imperial court down from the mountain, and the new city began to grow rapidly. He allocated land to his nobles to build their own houses, and work began on a grand new palace. The founding of Addis Ababa symbolized the beginning of a new, more settled and centralized era and an embrace of modernization that stood in stark contrast to the wandering courts of the past.

Menelik's reign was characterized by a voracious appetite for modernization. He was determined to introduce the technological and administrative tools that he believed would strengthen his empire and ensure its independence. He established the first modern ministries, a national currency, and a postal system. He was fascinated by new inventions and brought the first telephone and telegraph systems to the country. The most ambitious of these projects was the construction of a railway line to connect his landlocked capital with the French-controlled port of Djibouti on the coast. Work began in 1897, and while it was a massive and costly undertaking, Menelik understood that it was a vital lifeline for commerce and, more importantly, for the importation of modern arms.

By 1893, Menelik's patience with Italy had run out. Having consolidated his power, unified the major provinces under his rule, and built a formidable army, he no longer needed the pretense of an Italian alliance. He formally renounced the Treaty of Wuchale in its entirety, sending a letter to the European powers announcing his decision and denouncing Italy's duplicity. "Ethiopia is strong enough to maintain its independence," he declared, "and it does not care for any protectorate." The government in Rome was humiliated. Their attempt to acquire a vast African empire on the cheap, through a slyly worded treaty, had failed. For the politicians of the newly unified Italian state, national honor was now at stake. They came to believe that the only way to enforce their claim and salvage their prestige was through war.

The Italians began to reinforce their military position in Eritrea. They moved troops south of the Mareb River, which Menelik considered the legitimate border, and occupied the Tigrayan town of Adigrat. In late 1894, the Italian commander, General Oreste Baratieri, began to push deeper, defeating the forces of Ras Mengesha Yohannes at the Battle of Coatit in January 1895 and occupying the historic Tigrayan capital of Adwa. The Italian advance into the heartland of historic Christian Ethiopia was an act of aggression that could not be ignored.

Menelik responded with masterful patience and resolve. He spent months gathering the full strength of his empire. He issued a mobilization proclamation, a call to arms that resonated with centuries of Ethiopian tradition. "The enemy... is crossing the sea-gate that God has ordained for us," the proclamation read. "You, who are strong, help me with your strength. You, who are weak, help me with your prayers." From every province of his newly forged empire—Shewa, Tigray, Gojjam, and the recently conquered lands of the south—the great lords and their armies began the long march north. An army of unprecedented size, estimated at over one hundred thousand soldiers, was converging on Tigray. The diplomatic maneuvering was over. The stage was set for a decisive confrontation that would not only determine the fate of Ethiopia but would also send a shockwave across the entire colonized continent.

CHAPTER THIRTEEN: The Battle of Adwa: An African Victory

By the closing months of 1895, the great wager had been made. Emperor Menelik II, having formally repudiated the Treaty of Wuchale, had called the banners of his empire. From the newly conquered south and the ancient heartlands of the north, a vast river of humanity began to flow towards Tigray. This was not merely an army; it was a nation on the move. An estimated one hundred thousand soldiers, each accompanied by retainers, wives, and servants, marched north in a logistical operation of staggering scale, a testament to the organizational power of the restored imperial state. The great lords of the empire—Ras Mekonnen of Harar, Ras Mikael of Wollo, Ras Mengesha of Tigray, and Negus Tekle Haymanot of Gojjam—brought their powerful provincial armies to join the main force led by the emperor himself. Alongside Menelik rode the formidable Empress Taytu Betul, a shrewd strategist and a fierce patriot who commanded her own contingent and played a crucial role in the imperial war council.

The Italian commander in Eritrea, General Oreste Baratieri, watched this mobilization with a mixture of contempt and disbelief. He, like many Europeans of his day, was steeped in the racist conviction that an African army, no matter its size, was inherently inferior to a European one. He had modern artillery, disciplined brigades of Italian regulars, and thousands of well-trained Eritrean auxiliaries, or *askaris*, whom he considered the equal of any soldier. His intelligence, however, was poor, filtered through unreliable sources who consistently underestimated the size and resolve of the Ethiopian force. Baratieri was confident that the feudal Ethiopian host would prove to be a disorganized rabble, incapable of sustained operations and prone to disintegration at the first setback.

The first setback, however, was not Ethiopian. In early December 1895, a forward Italian column of around 2,500 men under the command of Major Pietro Toselli had pushed deep into Tigray, establishing an outpost on the flat-topped mountain of Amba Alagi. They were dangerously exposed. The Ethiopian vanguard, commanded by the brilliant Ras Mekonnen, Menelik's cousin and the governor of Harar, fell upon Toselli's isolated force with overwhelming numbers. On December 7th, in a furious battle, the Italian position was overrun. Toselli and the majority of his men were killed. The victory at Amba Alagi was a massive morale boost for the Ethiopians and a severe shock to the Italians. It proved that the Ethiopian army was not a rabble but a determined and capable fighting force.

Baratieri pulled his remaining forces back to a more defensible line, concentrating them around the town of Adigrat. He established a forward fort at Mekelle, which was soon surrounded by the main Ethiopian army. The siege of Mekelle, which began in early January 1896, was another revelation. The Ethiopians, possessing some modern artillery of their own, skillfully directed by Menelik and his generals, laid siege to the fort. For fifteen days they bombarded the Italian position, and crucially, they located and cut off the fort's only water supply, a feat attributed to the strategic counsel of Empress Taytu. With his garrison dying of thirst, the Italian commander had no choice but to surrender.

In a masterful act of psychological warfare, Menelik chose not to annihilate or imprison the surrendered garrison. Instead, he allowed the Italian commander, Major Galliano, and his one thousand two hundred men to march out of the fort with their arms and banners and rejoin Baratieri's main army. The gesture was calculated. It demonstrated Menelik's magnanimity and confidence, portraying him as a civilized monarch adhering to the rules of war. It also sowed discord among the Italians, as the returning soldiers brought with them sobering tales of the Ethiopian army's size, skill, and determination. Menelik's clemency was also a strategic play for a negotiated peace, but the Italians, stung by the defeats, were in no mood to talk.

For the next month, the two armies faced each other in a tense standoff near Adwa. It was a war of nerves and logistics. Menelik's massive army was a challenge to supply, but it was operating in its own country, able to draw sustenance from the surrounding land and from vast supply trains organized by the empress. Baratieri's army, by contrast, was at the end of a long, tenuous supply line stretching back to the coast. His resources were dwindling, and his men were becoming demoralized. The emperor's strategy was one of patient waiting, a *Fabian* strategy of letting the enemy exhaust himself. He knew that time was on his side.

In Rome, however, time was running out for Prime Minister Francesco Crispi. His government's aggressive colonial policy was under fire, and he desperately needed a glorious military victory to shore up his political position. He grew increasingly impatient with Baratieri's inaction, failing to appreciate the dire logistical situation his general faced. In late February, Crispi sent a now-infamous telegram to Baratieri, goading him with accusations of military incompetence and inaction. "This is a military phthisis, not a war," Crispi fumed, essentially accusing his general of cowardice. Humiliated and pressured, Baratieri knew he had to act. Faulty intelligence reports suggesting that Menelik's army was beginning to disperse due to lack of food sealed his decision. Against his own better judgment, he decided to risk everything on a single, decisive attack.

On the evening of February 29, 1896, a leap year, General Baratieri gave the order to advance. His plan was ambitious and fatally complex. He intended to move his army of approximately seventeen thousand seven hundred men, equipped with fifty-six artillery pieces, under the cover of darkness. The goal was not to launch a frontal assault on the main Ethiopian camp, but to occupy a series of hills on what he thought was strong defensive terrain, hoping to tempt Menelik into attacking him in a position of his own choosing. The army was divided into three brigades, commanded by Generals Matteo Albertone, Giuseppe Arimondi, and Vittorio Dabormida, with a fourth brigade held in reserve. Each brigade was to march independently through the night and converge at dawn on a designated set of hills. The success of the entire operation depended on precise timing, perfect coordination, and accurate maps, none of which the Italians possessed.

The advance was a disaster from the start. The terrain around Adwa was a chaotic labyrinth of steep, interlocking hills and treacherous, hidden valleys. The maps were hopelessly inaccurate. In the pitch-black darkness, the separate columns immediately lost their way. General Albertone's brigade, which was composed largely of the Eritrean askaris, marched too far and too fast, outstripping the other columns and veering off course. In the confusion, General Dabormida's brigade also went astray, while Arimondi's brigade was held up by the collision of two columns on a narrow track. By dawn on Sunday, March 1, the Italian army was not in a cohesive defensive line. It was hopelessly scattered, disoriented, and fragmented into isolated pockets across a wide and unforgiving landscape, miles from their intended positions.

The Ethiopians were completely unaware of the Italian maneuver until just before sunrise. Scouts from the command of Ras Alula, the veteran Tigrayan general, detected Albertone's isolated brigade advancing near the church of Enda Chidane Meret. The alarm was raised. Menelik was attending morning mass when the news arrived. His initial reaction was disbelief, but as more reports flooded in, it became clear that the Italians were not retreating but advancing to attack. The great lords of the empire converged on the emperor's tent. A momentous decision was made in minutes. The waiting was over. The Ethiopian army would give battle.

The cry went up through the vast Ethiopian camp: *"The spoiler has come, marching to rob us of our country!"* What followed was not a carefully orchestrated counter-attack, but the eruption of a nation's fury. From the camp, a tidal wave of humanity, a hundred thousand warriors, poured into the valleys to confront the invaders. They were armed with a mixture of modern rifles, old muskets, swords, and spears, but they were united by a common purpose and fought with a ferocity that stunned the Italians.

General Albertone's askari brigade was the first to be hit. Advancing alone, far ahead of the other columns, it was suddenly swamped by a massive Ethiopian force, including the armies of Negus Tekle Haymanot and Ras Mekonnen. The askaris fought with incredible bravery, holding their ground for hours against impossible odds, but their position was hopeless. They were surrounded and, by mid-morning, Albertone's brigade had ceased to exist. Albertone himself was captured.

As Arimondi's brigade advanced to try and support the disintegrating askari column, it too was met head-on by the main Ethiopian force, personally led by Emperor Menelik under the shadow of the great imperial red umbrella. The fighting centered on a hill known as Mount Belah. Empress Taytu, stationed nearby, hurled her own reserve of ten thousand men into the fray, urging them on with cries of "Courage! Strike them down! For your country and your faith!" The sheer weight of the Ethiopian numbers, combined with their fierce determination, proved irresistible. Arimondi's brigade was broken and overwhelmed. General Arimondi was killed, and his men fled in a desperate retreat.

Meanwhile, General Dabormida's brigade was fighting its own separate and doomed battle. Having lost all contact with the rest of the army, his column had descended into the narrow valley of Mariam Shavitu. There, it was encircled by the forces of Ras Mikael. For hours, Dabormida's men fought a desperate, heroic, but futile battle, completely unaware that the rest of the Italian army had already been defeated. Late in the afternoon, their ammunition exhausted, they were finally overrun. General Dabormida was killed, and his brigade was annihilated.

By midday, the battle was over. The modern, disciplined European army had been utterly routed. The Italian retreat became a desperate flight for survival as soldiers, broken and terrified, scrambled back towards Eritrea, harried by Ethiopian soldiers and by local peasants who rose up to take their revenge on the fleeing invaders. The Ethiopian victory was total and catastrophic for Italy.

The cost of victory was immense. Out of an army of under eighteen thousand, Italy suffered roughly seven thousand killed, one thousand five hundred wounded, and three thousand taken prisoner. Ethiopian casualties were just as staggering, with estimates of the dead ranging from four thousand to seven thousand and many more thousands wounded. The valley of Adwa was a scene of unimaginable carnage.

The aftermath was grim. The Italian prisoners were, for the most part, treated reasonably well, though they suffered greatly on the long march south to Addis Ababa. The fate of the captured Eritrean askaris, however, was brutal. Viewed as traitors who had taken up arms against their own people on behalf of a foreign invader, they were subjected to a traditional and terrible punishment. Some eight hundred had their right hand and left foot amputated. It was a stark message that collaboration with the enemy would not be tolerated.

News of the defeat at Adwa hit Italy like a thunderclap. It was a national humiliation of the highest order, the worst colonial disaster suffered by any European power in the 19th century. Riots erupted in major cities. The public outcry was so great that Prime Minister Crispi's government collapsed. The Italian dream of an Ethiopian empire was dead. On October 26, 1896, Italy signed the Treaty of Addis Ababa. In this document, Italy annulled the Treaty of Wuchale and unequivocally recognized the absolute sovereignty and independence of Ethiopia.

The Battle of Adwa was more than just a military victory; it was a pivotal moment in modern history. At the height of the European Scramble for Africa, while the rest of the continent was being carved up and colonized, Ethiopia had decisively defended its freedom. The victory resonated far beyond its borders, becoming a beacon of hope and a powerful symbol of African resistance for colonized peoples everywhere and for the burgeoning Pan-African movement. Menelik II had not only saved his nation; he had secured Ethiopia's unique place as the sole African power to successfully defeat a European colonial army and preserve its independence.

CHAPTER FOURTEEN: The Early Reign of Haile Selassie: Modernization and Centralization

The thunderous victory at Adwa had secured Ethiopia's independence, but it had not solved the fundamental question of how to govern a vast, diverse, and feudal empire in a world of rapidly modernizing colonial powers. Emperor Menelik II had been the architect of both the victory and the modern Ethiopian state, a ruler whose personal authority held the sprawling empire together. But as the 20th century dawned, the great emperor began to fail. A series of strokes, beginning in 1909, left him incapacitated, a silent and paralyzed figure in his own palace. The immense power he had wielded was now up for grabs, and the country held its breath, waiting to see if the unified state he had forged would survive him.

Menelik's chosen heir was his grandson, Lij Iyasu. The boy, a teenager at the time of Menelik's incapacitation, was the son of Menelik's daughter Shewa Regga and Ras Mikael, the powerful Oromo leader of Wollo whom Yohannes IV had forcibly converted to Christianity. Iyasu's lineage was a deliberate political choice by Menelik, an attempt to bridge the gap between the dominant Christian Amhara-Tigrayan elite and the large Muslim Oromo population that had been incorporated into the empire. Upon Menelik's death in December 1913, the young Iyasu V ascended to the throne, though he was never formally crowned. He was a radical departure from the emperors who had preceded him. He was young, restless, and contemptuous of the rigid protocols of the Shewan court. He refused to be confined to the palace in Addis Ababa, spending most of his time traveling throughout the empire, particularly in the eastern and southern provinces.

Iyasu's reign was a direct challenge to the established order. He seemed intent on dismantling the system of Shewan Amhara dominance that Menelik had institutionalized. He courted the empire's marginalized peoples, showing a marked preference for the company of the Oromo, the Afar, and the Somalis. Most alarmingly to the conservative Christian establishment, he openly embraced his Muslim heritage. He took multiple wives from prominent Muslim families, built mosques, and was rumored to have privately converted to Islam, a charge he never publicly refuted. He was seen wearing the turban of a Muslim emir and participating in their religious festivals. For his supporters, this was a revolutionary attempt to create a more inclusive, multicultural Ethiopian identity. For the powerful Shewan aristocracy and the Orthodox Church, it was heresy and treason. They saw an emperor who was systematically alienating his Christian power base and, by forging ties with Somali leaders like Mohammed Abdullah Hassan (dubbed the "Mad Mullah" by the British), dangerously aligning Ethiopia with anti-colonial Islamic movements at the height of the First World War.

The Shewan elite, led by Menelik's aging and influential Minister of War, Fitawrari Habte Giyorgis Dinagde, decided that the emperor had to go. In September 1916, while Iyasu was away in Harar, the nobles gathered in Addis Ababa. They secured the support of Abuna Mattewos, the head of the Orthodox Church, who formally released the nation from its oath of allegiance to Iyasu and excommunicated him. The plotters proclaimed Menelik's daughter, Zewditu, as Empress. Iyasu, caught off guard, tried to rally support, and his father, Ras Mikael, marched south from Wollo with a large army to defend his son's throne. However, at the Battle of Segale in October 1916, Mikael's army was decisively crushed by the main Shewan force. Mikael was captured and paraded through the streets of the capital in chains. Iyasu himself escaped, spending the next five years as a fugitive before being captured and imprisoned. His brief, turbulent, and revolutionary reign was over.

The coup of 1916 did not produce a single, clear ruler. It created a unique and often tense political arrangement known as the diarchy. The new Empress Zewditu was a deeply pious and conservative woman, respected as the daughter of the great Menelik but with little interest in the day-to-day business of government. She became the symbolic head of the state, representing the traditional, isolationist, and religious wing of the court. Real executive power was placed in the hands of a Regent and Heir Apparent: the 24-year-old Ras Tafari Makonnen.

Tafari was the son of Ras Mekonnen, the hero of Adwa and Menelik's cousin. He was a man of a completely different temperament from the empress. He was cool, calculating, highly intelligent, and possessed of a boundless ambition that was masked by a quiet, unassuming demeanor. He was the undisputed leader of the small but growing party of "young Ethiopians," a group of modernizers who believed that the country's survival depended on a rapid program of political, social, and technological reform. The next fourteen years would be defined by the subtle, and sometimes not-so-subtle, power struggle between the conservative faction loyal to Empress Zewditu and the progressive faction led by the ambitious young Regent.

Ras Tafari understood that his primary challenge was the deeply entrenched power of the great provincial lords. The regional *mesafint*, though subdued by Menelik, still ruled their domains as semi-independent kings, commanding their own armies and collecting their own taxes. Tafari's entire political project was aimed at breaking their power and centralizing all authority in the capital, and ultimately, in his own hands. His second, related goal was to modernize the country, not for its own sake, but as a means of strengthening the state and guaranteeing its independence against the ever-present threat of European colonialism. To achieve this, he realized he needed to integrate Ethiopia into the new international system that was emerging after the First World War.

His first major diplomatic triumph was securing Ethiopia's admission into the League of Nations in 1923. It was a brilliant move, a calculated step to place Ethiopia on an equal footing with the sovereign nations of the world and to gain an international forum where any future aggression could be challenged. The application was met with stiff resistance, particularly from Great Britain and its dominions, who argued that Ethiopia was not fit to join the community of "civilized" nations because of the persistence of slavery and the slave trade within its borders. The charge was true; a vast system of domestic slavery, known as the *gabbar* system, was a core feature of the imperial economy, particularly in the newly conquered southern territories. To overcome this opposition, Tafari launched a skillful diplomatic campaign. He argued that membership in the League would strengthen his hand against the conservative nobles who supported the practice, and just before the final vote, he issued a decree officially outlawing the slave trade and providing for the gradual emancipation of slaves. It was a promise that would prove difficult to enforce, but it was enough. Ethiopia was admitted, and Tafari had won a major victory, enhancing both his country's security and his own international prestige.

At home, Tafari's modernizing agenda advanced slowly, always in the face of conservative opposition. He understood the power of modern education as a tool for creating a new generation of administrators loyal to the central government rather than to their regional lords. He established the first modern government school in the capital, the Tafari Makonnen School, in 1925, staffing it with foreign teachers. He hand-picked promising young men and sent them to be educated in Europe and America, creating a new, foreign-educated elite who would form the nucleus of his modern bureaucracy. This was a direct threat to the old nobility and the church, who saw their traditional monopoly on education and administration being eroded.

He also worked to create a modern military. The national army was still a feudal levy, a collection of personal armies loyal to their individual lords. Tafari began to build a small, modern imperial bodyguard, the *Kebur Zabagna*, equipped with modern weapons and trained by European military advisors. This force was loyal only to him and the central state. He also introduced a new tax system, attempting to have taxes paid in cash directly to the central treasury, bypassing the regional lords who traditionally collected tribute in kind for their own enrichment. Each of these reforms was a careful, deliberate step to chip away at the foundations of the old feudal order.

The conservative faction, centered around Empress Zewditu, viewed these changes with deep suspicion. They saw Tafari's embrace of foreign advisors, his promotion of Western education, and his diplomatic engagement with Europe as a betrayal of Ethiopian tradition and a dangerous opening for foreign influence. The empress herself frequently acted to slow or block his proposals. The most powerful figure in the conservative camp was the old war minister, Fitawrari Habte Giyorgis Dinagde. For years, he held the balance of power, a respected link to the era of Menelik, sometimes supporting the Regent, sometimes the Empress. His death in 1926 removed a major obstacle from Tafari's path and destabilized the delicate political balance.

With Habte Giyorgis gone, the political struggle intensified. In 1928, after quashing a minor palace coup aimed at removing him, Tafari made a bold move. He pressured the empress and the assembled nobility to grant him the title of *Negus*, or King. This was a significant promotion. While Zewditu remained Empress, Tafari was now no longer just a regent, but a crowned king in his own right, ruling alongside her. The elevation of Tafari was a clear signal that the balance of power had shifted decisively in his favor, and it was the final provocation for the most powerful remaining conservatives.

The standard of rebellion was raised by the man who had the most to lose from Tafari's rise: Ras Gugsa Welle. Ras Gugsa was the governor of the powerful northern province of Begemder, a nobleman of the old school, and, most importantly, the estranged husband of Empress Zewditu herself. He saw Tafari as a dangerous usurper who was destroying the religious and social fabric of the empire. He saw himself as the champion of the true Ethiopia, the defender of the Empress and the Orthodox faith. In early 1930, he declared his intention to march on the capital and rid the court of Tafari and his "satanic" modernizing ways. He gathered a large, traditional army and began his advance south.

The confrontation that followed was the final, decisive battle between the old Ethiopia and the new. The Battle of Anchem, fought on March 31, 1930, was less a battle than a demonstration of technology. Ras Gugsa's army was a magnificent feudal host, a thirty-five-thousand-man force of charging cavalry and swordsmen. Tafari's army, commanded by his Minister of War, Ras Mulugeta Yeggazu, was smaller but represented the modern state. It had trained infantry, machine guns, and, crucially, a tiny air force consisting of a few biplanes. As Gugsa's army charged across the plain of Anchem, they were met not only with disciplined rifle and machine-gun fire but also with bombs dropped from the air. The psychological impact of the aircraft was devastating. The traditionalist army, which had never seen such a weapon, broke and fled. Ras Gugsa Welle refused to retreat and was killed in the fighting.

The victory was absolute. It was the death knell of the old feudal order and the triumph of the centralized, modernizing state that Tafari had been patiently building for fourteen years. The news from the battlefield had barely reached the capital when, just two days later, on April 2, 1930, Empress Zewditu died. The official cause was illness, but the timing was so convenient that rumors of poison have persisted ever since. With the empress dead and her champion defeated on the battlefield, there were no obstacles left. Ras Tafari Makonnen was now the sole and undisputed master of Ethiopia.

On November 2, 1930, *Negus* Tafari was crowned Emperor of Ethiopia, taking the regnal name Haile Selassie I, meaning "Power of the Trinity." The coronation was an event of unparalleled magnificence, a carefully stage-managed piece of political theater designed for an international audience. Dignitaries from across the globe, including Britain's Duke of Gloucester, were invited to Addis Ababa to witness the elaborate ceremony, which blended ancient Ethiopian Christian rites with the pomp of a European coronation. The message was clear: Ethiopia was an ancient kingdom, but it was also a modern nation, a member of the international community, ruled by a sophisticated and forward-looking monarch.

To codify his victory and legally establish the new political order, Haile Selassie promulgated Ethiopia's first-ever written constitution in July 1931. On the surface, the document seemed to create a modern constitutional monarchy. It established a bicameral parliament, with a Senate and a Chamber of Deputies, and outlined the duties of government ministers. It was a document designed to impress the outside world. In reality, the 1931 Constitution was an instrument of absolute power. The members of both houses were not elected but appointed by the Emperor. The parliament had no real power; it could only advise. The constitution's primary purpose was to legally transfer all power away from the regional nobility and concentrate it in the person of the Emperor. Article 6 stated that "the person of the Emperor is sacred, his dignity is inviolable and his power is indisputable." The era of the princes was legally, as well as militarily, at an end. Haile Selassie had finally achieved the goal he had pursued for a decade and a half: the creation of a centralized state under his absolute control.

CHAPTER FIFTEEN: The Italian Invasion and Occupation (1935–1941)

The coronation of Haile Selassie I had been a spectacle of hope, a declaration to the world that Ethiopia was embracing modernity on its own terms. The new Emperor's centralizing reforms and his skillful diplomacy at the League of Nations were designed to secure the nation's future in an increasingly dangerous world. But in Europe, a different kind of modernization was taking hold. In Italy, Benito Mussolini and his Fascist party were nursing a forty-year-old wound. The name "Adwa" was not a symbol of African pride but a stain on Italian honor, a humiliating defeat that had to be avenged. Mussolini dreamed of a new Roman Empire, a vast colonial domain that would project Italian power and prestige. Ethiopia, the nation that had so spectacularly defied Italy's first imperial ambitions, was the essential, symbolic prize. The stage was being set for a clash between two profoundly different visions of national destiny: one of an ancient African kingdom struggling to modernize and maintain its freedom, the other of a modern European power determined to subjugate it.

Mussolini's intentions were thinly veiled. He began a massive military buildup in the Italian colonies of Eritrea to the north and Somaliland to the south, pouring in soldiers, heavy artillery, tanks, and aircraft. All he needed was a pretext for war, an incident that could be manufactured to portray Ethiopia as the aggressor. That pretext arrived on December 5, 1934, at the Walwal oasis in the Ogaden desert. Walwal was a collection of wells in a remote, ill-defined border region, territory that was indisputably Ethiopian according to treaty but had been quietly garrisoned by the Italians. When an Anglo-Ethiopian boundary commission arrived at the oasis, they found it occupied by an Italian-led force of Somali colonial troops, or *banda*. The Ethiopian escort, under the command of Fitaurari Shiferra Balcha, demanded that the Italians withdraw. The Italians refused. A tense standoff ensued, and after two weeks, a shot was fired—it is unclear by which side—and a brief, bloody skirmish erupted. The Italians, with their superior firepower, including two aircraft, easily repulsed the Ethiopians.

For Mussolini, the Walwal Incident was a godsend. Ignoring the fact that the clash had occurred eighty kilometers inside Ethiopian territory, he immediately accused Ethiopia of unprovoked aggression. He demanded a formal apology, a salute to the Italian flag, and a massive indemnity. Emperor Haile Selassie, a veteran of international diplomacy, refused to be baited. He calmly replied that since the question of sovereignty over the oasis was in dispute, the matter should be settled not by threats, but by impartial arbitration under the terms of a 1928 Italo-Ethiopian treaty of friendship. Italy rejected the offer out of hand. Mussolini had no interest in arbitration; he wanted a war, and Walwal was his excuse.

Haile Selassie put his faith in the institution he had worked so hard to join: the League of Nations. In January 1935, Ethiopia formally appealed to the League under Article 11 of its Covenant, which dealt with actions that threatened to disturb international peace. It was the first true test of the League's principle of collective security, a test it would spectacularly fail. The dominant powers in the League, Britain and France, were paralyzed by their own strategic anxieties. Their primary foreign policy goal was to contain the growing threat of Adolf Hitler's Germany. They saw Mussolini's Italy as a vital counterweight to Germany and were desperate to keep him as an ally. In April 1935, they met with Mussolini at Stresa in Italy to form a common front against German rearmament. In their eagerness to secure this "Stresa Front," the fate of Ethiopia was a secondary, inconvenient concern. Behind the scenes, they signaled to Mussolini that they would not stand in his way, implicitly giving him a green light for his African adventure.

Throughout the spring and summer of 1935, the League dithered. It appointed commissions and heard reports, but took no meaningful action. As Italy's military buildup continued in plain sight, the Emperor's pleas grew more desperate. "Is it the Council's intention to sit by until the sword is drawn?" the

Ethiopian delegate asked in Geneva. The answer, effectively, was yes. The League did eventually impose sanctions on Italy after the invasion began, but they were a cynical and useless gesture. The sanctions banned the export of arms to Italy, but crucially excluded oil, steel, and coal—the very materials needed to fuel a modern war machine. The Suez Canal, the vital artery through which Mussolini supplied his invasion force, remained open to Italian shipping. The great powers had chosen appeasement, sacrificing the sovereignty of one of their own members in the vain hope of placating a dictator.

On the morning of October 3, 1935, the wait was over. Without a declaration of war, 100,000 Italian soldiers under the command of General Emilio De Bono crossed the Mareb River from Eritrea and marched into Tigray. From the south, a smaller force under General Rodolfo Graziani pushed into the Ogaden from Italian Somaliland. The Second Italo-Ethiopian War had begun. The disparity in force was immense. Italy had mobilized one of the most powerful armies ever deployed in a colonial conflict, a force that would eventually swell to over half a million men. It was a modern, mechanized army with tanks, armored cars, motorized transport, and, most critically, a powerful air force, the *Regia Aeronautica*.

The Ethiopian army, by contrast, was a magnificent but anachronistic feudal host. Menelik's mobilization for Adwa forty years earlier was re-enacted, as the great provincial lords, the *rases*, answered the Emperor's call and brought their personal armies to the front. It was a force of immense courage and patriotism, but it was hopelessly outgunned. While the Emperor's elite Imperial Guard was well-trained and equipped with modern rifles, the vast majority of the soldiers were armed with antiquated firearms, spears, and swords. They had almost no anti-aircraft guns and no air force to challenge Italian supremacy in the skies.

The initial Italian advance was slow and methodical. De Bono, a cautious commander, captured the historic towns of Adwa and Aksum with little resistance, pausing to build roads and supply depots. The fall of Adwa, the site of the great victory of 1896, was a bitter psychological blow for the Ethiopians and a moment of ecstatic triumph for the Italians. In Addis Ababa, Haile Selassie worked feverishly to organize a counter-offensive. He devised an ambitious plan for a multi-pronged attack on the Italian northern front, a "Christmas Offensive," hoping to catch the invaders off guard.

The offensive, launched in December 1935, showed the tenacity of the Ethiopian soldier. The armies of Ras Imru Haile Selassie and Ras Seyoum Mengesha scored some notable early successes, inflicting heavy casualties on the Italians and their Eritrean askari auxiliaries. At the Battle of Dembeguina Pass, Ras Imru's forces outmaneuvered and nearly destroyed an entire Italian column. But these victories were fleeting. The Ethiopians could win localized battles, but they could not win the war. Italian air power was the decisive factor. Whenever Ethiopian forces massed for an attack, Italian aircraft would appear, bombing and strafing them with impunity, shattering their formations and their morale.

Frustrated by De Bono's plodding pace, Mussolini replaced him in December with Marshal Pietro Badoglio, a more ruthless and aggressive commander. Badoglio was instructed to win the war quickly, by any means necessary. He immediately authorized the use of a weapon that was banned by the Geneva Protocol, to which Italy was a signatory: chemical weapons. Badoglio unleashed a reign of terror from the air, systematically dropping tons of mustard gas on Ethiopian combatants and civilians alike. This was not a limited, tactical use of gas; it was a deliberate strategy to terrorize a population and break the will of its armies.

The effects were horrific. Mustard gas is a blistering agent that causes agonizing burns to the skin, eyes, and respiratory tract. Ethiopian soldiers, with no gas masks or protective clothing, were completely defenseless. Italian pilots sprayed the deadly chemical "rain" over troop columns, villages, farms, and rivers. Red Cross field hospitals, clearly marked with the international symbol, were deliberately targeted. Survivors told of men and animals blinded and screaming in agony, their skin covered in horrific, suppurating blisters. The gas contaminated water supplies and grazing land, poisoning those who were not hit directly. This chemical warfare was a war crime of immense proportions, and it had its intended effect. The morale of the Ethiopian armies on the northern front began to crumble under this invisible, agonizing onslaught.

By the spring of 1936, the Ethiopian position was becoming desperate. With his northern armies disintegrating, Haile Selassie decided to risk everything on one last, desperate gamble. He gathered the last great Ethiopian field army, a force of around thirty thousand men centered on his elite Imperial Guard, and marched north to lead the attack himself. He planned a frontal assault on the main Italian army, which was dug in at Maychew in southern Tigray. It was a courageous but suicidal plan, pitting the last of Ethiopia's finest soldiers against an entrenched enemy with overwhelming superiority in artillery and air power.

The Battle of Maychew, fought on March 31, 1936, was the Adwa of this new, terrible war, but with the outcome tragically reversed. For hours, the men of the Imperial Guard, led by the Emperor in person, hurled themselves against the Italian lines with incredible bravery. They broke through the first line of defense and nearly overran the Italian artillery positions. But courage alone could not overcome machine guns, heavy artillery, and relentless aerial bombardment. By the afternoon, the attack had stalled. As the exhausted Ethiopians began to fall back, the Italians unleashed a devastating counter-attack, supported by a massive chemical weapons bombardment. The Imperial Guard was not just defeated; it was annihilated. The last organized Ethiopian army was shattered.

The road to the capital was now open. Haile Selassie managed to escape the battlefield and began a harrowing retreat back to Addis Ababa. The remnants of his army were harried every step of the way by Italian aircraft and by hostile local populations who rose up against the defeated emperor. He arrived in his capital on April 30th to find it in a state of panic and chaos. He convened a council of his remaining nobles to decide on a course of action. It was the most agonizing decision of his life. Some urged him to stay and lead a guerrilla resistance from the countryside, to fight to the death in the tradition of his ancestors. Others, including Ras Kassa Hailu, argued that the only hope was for him to leave the country and make a personal appeal to the conscience of the world at the League of Nations. A dead emperor was a martyr; a living emperor in exile was a symbol of continued sovereignty.

With a heavy heart, Haile Selassie chose exile. On May 2, 1936, he, his family, and a small retinue boarded a train for the port of Djibouti. His departure signaled the collapse of the government. Law and order in Addis Ababa broke down completely as mobs looted the city, including the imperial palace. Three days later, on May 5th, Marshal Badoglio's motorized columns entered the capital. From a balcony in Rome, Benito Mussolini announced to a vast, cheering crowd that the war was over. "Ethiopia is Italian!" he roared. He declared the birth of a new Roman Empire and that King Victor Emmanuel III of Italy was now also the Emperor of Ethiopia. To the outside world, it seemed that the last independent nation in Africa had finally been extinguished.

The Italian occupation of Ethiopia lasted five years, from 1936 to 1941. It was not the glorious imperial project of fascist propaganda, but a brutal and unstable military rule over a resentful and rebellious population. The Italians attempted to impose a rigid system of racial segregation, a form of apartheid, creating separate residential areas, shops, and transport for whites and blacks. They pursued a policy of *divide et impera*, attempting to dismantle the Amhara-dominated unitary state by creating separate administrative regions for the Oromo, Somali, and other groups, and by favoring Islam over Orthodox Christianity.

The conventional war may have been lost, but Ethiopian resistance was far from over. Almost immediately, a guerrilla movement of patriots, the *Arbegnoch*, sprang up across the country. In the west, the remnants of Ras Imru's army continued to fight. In the central highlands, nobles and commoners alike took to the mountains to wage a campaign of raids and ambushes against the occupiers. The Italian response was savage. The new viceroy, Marshal Rodolfo Graziani, a man who had earned the nickname "the Butcher of

Fezzan" for his brutal campaigns in Libya, was determined to crush the resistance through terror.

The defining moment of Graziani's reign of terror came on February 19, 1937, a date known in Ethiopia as *Yekatit 12*. During a public ceremony in Addis Ababa celebrating the birth of an Italian prince, two young Eritreans, Abraha Deboch and Moges Asgedom, threw a volley of grenades at the stage where Graziani and other fascist dignitaries were standing. Graziani was wounded, but survived. The reprisal was immediate and horrific. For the next three days, fascist Blackshirt squads, armed with clubs, knives, and gasoline, went on a murderous rampage through the city. They slaughtered thousands of innocent Ethiopians in their homes and on the streets. They specifically targeted the educated elite—those who had been educated abroad, who could speak foreign languages, who were seen as the potential leaders of a future independent Ethiopia.

The violence was not confined to the capital. Following the massacre, Graziani ordered the execution of the monks at the ancient and revered monastery of Debre Libanos, whom he wrongly suspected of complicity in the plot. Over three hundred monks and deacons were rounded up and shot. Far from crushing the resistance, the atrocities of *Yekatit 12* and Debre Libanos horrified the Ethiopian people, fueled their hatred of the occupiers, and swelled the ranks of the *Arbegnoch*. The guerrilla war intensified, rendering Italian control insecure outside the main towns and fortified posts.

Meanwhile, in exile, Haile Selassie became a living symbol of the world's failure to stand up to fascist aggression. On June 30, 1936, he delivered a powerful and prophetic speech before the Assembly of the League of Nations in Geneva. Speaking in Amharic, his quiet dignity and somber warnings captivated the world. He described the horror of the chemical weapon attacks on his people and chastised the great powers for their inaction. "It is us today. It will be you tomorrow," he warned. His speech was a moral triumph but a diplomatic failure. Shortly afterward, the League voted to lift the meaningless sanctions on Italy, officially recognizing the Italian conquest. For the next few years, Haile Selassie lived in quiet exile in Bath, England, a largely forgotten figure as the world lurched towards a much larger conflict.

The start of the Second World War in September 1939, and particularly Italy's entry into the war on the side of Nazi Germany in June 1940, dramatically changed the strategic picture. Suddenly, Italian East Africa was no longer an isolated colonial possession; it was a dagger pointed at the British Empire's vital sea lanes in the Red Sea and the Suez Canal. Ethiopia's long, lonely struggle was now part of a global war against fascism. The Ethiopian Patriots were no longer just rebels; they were valuable allies. The British government, which had once turned its back on the Emperor, now saw him as a key asset.

In January 1941, the British launched the East African Campaign, a major offensive to drive the Italians out of the Horn of Africa. It was a multi-pronged attack. One force advanced from Sudan, another from Kenya. Crucially, a third front was opened from within Ethiopia itself. On January 20, 1941, Haile Selassie was flown from Sudan back across the border into his homeland. He was accompanied by a small but elite British-led unit known as Gideon Force, commanded by the eccentric but brilliant Major Orde Wingate. Their mission was not to defeat the Italian army, which still numbered nearly 300,000 men, but to act as a catalyst for a full-scale national uprising, coordinating the activities of the thousands of *Arbegnoch* fighters, who were now armed and supplied by the British. The liberation of Ethiopia had begun.

CHAPTER SIXTEEN: Liberation and the Return of the Emperor

The dawn of 1941 found Ethiopia in the fifth year of a brutal occupation, a nation subjugated but not subdued. Across the rugged highlands, the guerrilla fighters known as the *Arbegnoch* waged a relentless shadow war, keeping the flame of resistance alive. In his quiet exile in England, Emperor Haile Selassie had become a symbol of a lost cause, a king without a kingdom. But the geopolitical chessboard had been violently overturned. Italy's entry into the Second World War on the side of Nazi Germany had transformed the East African theater from a colonial backwater into a strategic front. The British Empire, now fighting for its own survival, saw the Italian presence in the Horn of Africa as a grave threat to its lifeline through the Suez Canal. The forgotten Emperor and his tenacious Patriots were suddenly indispensable allies. The stage was set for one of the most remarkable campaigns of the war, a multi-pronged offensive that would not only liberate a nation but would also restore its sovereign to the throne.

The British plan for the East African Campaign was a masterpiece of strategic envelopment. It called for a massive, three-front assault on Mussolini's African empire. From the north, a formidable force of British and Indian divisions under Lieutenant-General William Platt would push south from Sudan into the heart of the Italian colony of Eritrea. From the south, Lieutenant-General Alan Cunningham would lead a fast-moving army of South African, Nigerian, and other African colonial troops out of Kenya, sweeping through Italian Somaliland and then racing north towards the Ethiopian capital. The third front, however, was a different beast altogether. It was smaller, more unconventional, and of immense symbolic importance. It would be a spearhead of liberation thrust directly into the Ethiopian heartland of Gojjam. Its purpose was not to conquer territory but to ignite a national insurrection. At its head was the returning Emperor, Haile Selassie.

On January 20, 1941, the Emperor's personal standard was raised once more on Ethiopian soil. He crossed the border from Sudan and established a temporary camp at the village of Omedla. He was not alone. Accompanying him was a small, bizarre, but highly effective military unit known as Gideon Force. Commanded by the eccentric, brilliant, and ferociously pro-Ethiopian British officer, Major Orde Wingate, Gideon Force was a motley collection of about eight hundred Sudanese and Ethiopian regulars, supported by a handful of British officers and NCOs. Wingate, a devout Christian and a master of irregular warfare, saw the campaign in biblical terms. He was leading a righteous army to restore a Christian king to his throne. His mission, as he saw it, was not to defeat the Italian army—which outnumbered his tiny force by more than forty to one in the region—but to serve as the military and political catalyst for a massive uprising of the *Arbegnoch*. He was the grit in the oyster, the irritant around which the pearl of a national liberation would form.

The Emperor's presence had an immediate and electric effect. For five years, the Patriots had fought in isolated bands, their resistance a testament to their courage but lacking a central, unifying figure. Now, the Lion of Judah had returned. Messengers fanned out across the highlands, carrying the news that the *Negusa Nagast* was back in his kingdom. From their mountain strongholds, Patriot leaders like Belay Zeleke in Gojjam and Ras Abebe Aregai in Shewa rallied their followers to join the cause. Gideon Force began its audacious march into Gojjam, its primary weapon not its mortars and machine guns, but the very presence of the Emperor. Their strategy was one of lethal disruption. They ambushed Italian columns, attacked remote garrisons, and, most importantly, armed and coordinated the thousands of Patriot fighters who flocked to the Emperor's banner.

While Wingate and the Emperor were lighting the fires of rebellion in the west, the main British military campaigns were proceeding with astonishing speed. In the south, General Cunningham's offensive was a textbook example of a modern blitzkrieg. His motorized columns smashed through the Italian defenses in Somaliland, capturing the port of Mogadishu on

February 25. Instead of pausing, Cunningham made the audacious decision to turn his army north and dash for the Ethiopian capital, a thousand miles away across the arid Ogaden. Italian morale, already brittle after years of being harassed by guerrillas, collapsed completely. The Italian army in the south did not fight; it dissolved. Many of the colonial troops, with little loyalty to their Italian officers, deserted en masse.

In the north, General Platt's advance was a much tougher proposition. The Italians had turned the mountains of Eritrea into a fortress. At the town of Keren, a formidable Italian army, under the command of the capable General Nicolangelo Carnimeo, was dug into a seemingly impregnable network of mountain peaks and fortified passes. For eight long weeks, from early February to the end of March 1941, British and Indian troops fought one of the most brutal and heroic battles of the war. In a series of bloody frontal assaults against fortified ridges, they slowly and at great cost dislodged the Italian defenders. The Battle of Keren was a slogging match that broke the back of the best Italian forces in East Africa. After Keren fell on March 27, the road to Asmara and the Eritrean port of Massawa was open. The northern pincer was closing.

As the two main British armies advanced, Gideon Force continued its surreal and spectacular campaign in Gojjam. Wingate, leading from the front with a Bible in one hand and a rifle in the other, seemed to be everywhere at once, orchestrating a symphony of chaos against the Italian garrisons. His small force, amplified by thousands of Patriots, tied down tens of thousands of Italian troops who could have been used to stem the tide of Cunningham's advance. In early March, they laid siege to the Italian fort at Bure. After a week of fighting, the Italian garrison of several thousand men, unnerved by the ferocity of the Patriots and by the news of the British advances elsewhere, abandoned the fort and fled.

The next major objective was Debre Marqos, the capital of Gojjam. Here, the Italian commander, Colonel Natale, commanded a force of over twelve thousand men. Wingate, with his tiny Gideon Force and a growing but still undisciplined Patriot army, could not hope to take the town by conventional assault. Instead, he launched a campaign of bluff and psychological warfare. He used his few mortars to create the illusion of a major artillery bombardment and sent fabricated messages designed to be intercepted, hinting at the imminent arrival of a non-existent British armored division. The deception worked. Convinced he was about to be overwhelmed, and with his lines of retreat threatened, Colonel Natale abandoned Debre Marqos and began a desperate fighting retreat towards the relative safety of Addis Ababa. Wingate and his Patriots had captured a provincial capital, effectively liberating Gojjam with a force that was little more than a battalion strong.

By early April, the Italian position in Ethiopia was hopeless. With Platt's army advancing from the north and Cunningham's columns racing up from the south, the Viceroy and Commander-in-Chief, Prince Amedeo, the Duke of Aosta, declared Addis Ababa an open city to save it from destruction. On April 6, 1941, General Cunningham's South African armored cars rolled into the capital, taking the formal surrender of the city. The main prize had fallen with barely a shot fired. The British established a military administration, officially designated as the Occupied Enemy Territory Administration (OETA). To them, Ethiopia was a conquered Italian colony that now had to be administered by its new military masters. This perspective was about to collide head-on with that of the Emperor.

Haile Selassie and Orde Wingate were furious. They had been fighting to liberate a sovereign nation, not to see it transferred from one form of foreign control to another. Wingate had deliberately orchestrated the Emperor's advance as a slow, dignified, and sovereign march towards his own capital, liberating his own people along the way. Now, Cunningham had captured the city and was treating it as enemy property. A tense political struggle ensued. The British administrators, many of whom were colonial veterans with a low opinion of African self-governance, wanted to establish what amounted to a protectorate. They argued that the country was too chaotic and disorganized to govern itself. The Emperor, however, was adamant. He was not a conquered subject; he was a victorious ally, the legitimate ruler of a sovereign state.

After weeks of tense negotiation, the Emperor won. The British government, recognizing the political importance of honoring their commitment to the man who had become a global symbol of resistance to fascism, overruled the local administrators. The Emperor would be allowed to enter his capital and reassume his throne. The date chosen for his return was one of immense symbolic weight: May 5, 1941. It was exactly five years to the day that Marshal Badoglio and the Italian Fascists had entered Addis Ababa in triumph.

The return was a moment of profound and cathartic joy for the Ethiopian people. Crowds lined the streets as the Emperor's motorcade made its way to the old Menelik Palace. He was a small, dignified figure, but he represented the restoration of a nation's pride. He stepped onto the balcony and delivered a speech that has become one of the most famous in Ethiopian history. It was a speech not of vengeance, but of reconciliation and forward-looking resolve. "Today is the day on which we have vanquished our enemy," he proclaimed. "Therefore, when we say let us rejoice with our hearts, let not our rejoicing be in any other way but in the spirit of Christ. Do not return evil for evil. Do not indulge in the atrocities which the enemy has been practicing in his usual way, even to the last." He called on his people to welcome the defeated Italians, to show them mercy, and to focus on the immense task of rebuilding their devastated country.

The capture of Addis Ababa and the return of the Emperor did not, however, mark the end of the war. The Duke of Aosta had withdrawn the main remnants of the Italian army to the formidable mountain fortress of Amba Alagi in the north. This was the same location where the Italians had been defeated in 1895, and the Duke, a cousin of the Italian king, was determined to make a final, honorable stand. For three weeks in May, a combined force of British, Indian, South African, and Ethiopian Patriot forces laid siege to the mountain. Facing relentless artillery bombardment and with his water supply cut off, the Duke of Aosta finally surrendered on May 19. He was granted the full honors of war, in recognition of his chivalrous defense.

Even then, the fighting was not completely over. A determined Italian force of some forty thousand men under the command of General Guglielmo Nasi, one of the few Italian commanders who had earned the respect of his Ethiopian adversaries, held out in the region around Gondar. For another six months, Nasi's men waged a skillful and tenacious guerrilla campaign, launching raids from their mountain strongholds. It was not until November 27, 1941, that the last of these Italian forces finally surrendered, bringing the East African Campaign to its definitive end.

Haile Selassie was back on his throne, the sovereign ruler of a liberated Ethiopia. But the country he now governed was in ruins. The economy was shattered, the infrastructure was destroyed, and the five years of war and occupation had opened deep wounds in the fabric of the nation. The country was awash with weapons, and many of the Patriot leaders, who had fought for years with little to no central control, were not keen to simply hand over their newfound power and autonomy to a restored monarch in Addis Ababa. Furthermore, the Emperor's sovereignty was far from absolute. The British army remained in effective control of large parts of the country, and British administrators held key advisory positions in the new government. The struggle for Ethiopia's independence was not over; it had simply entered a new, more complex, and political phase.

CHAPTER SEVENTEEN: The Post-War Years and the Federation with Eritrea

On May 5, 1941, Emperor Haile Selassie returned to his capital, a symbol of a nation resurrected. The cheering crowds that welcomed him celebrated a victory that was profound and deeply felt, yet the country he now ruled was a shadow of the one he had left. Five years of war and occupation had left the economy in ruins, the administration in tatters, and the social fabric frayed. The joy of liberation was tempered by the stark reality of the immense task ahead: rebuilding a shattered nation while navigating a new and complex geopolitical landscape. The Emperor was back on his throne, but he was far from being the absolute master of his own house.

His first and most immediate challenge was the continued presence of his liberators. The British army, having swept the Italians out of East Africa, had established the Occupied Enemy Territory Administration (OETA). From their perspective, they had conquered an Italian colony, and it was now their responsibility to administer it. The Emperor and his fledgling government were, in the eyes of many British officers, little more than a native authority to be managed. This paternalistic attitude created immediate friction. Haile Selassie had not fought for five years to exchange one master for another. He was a victorious ally and the sovereign of an independent state, and he was determined to make the British acknowledge it.

The tense relationship was codified in the Anglo-Ethiopian Agreement of 1942. It was a bitter pill for the Emperor to swallow. While the agreement formally recognized Ethiopia's sovereignty, it granted Britain extraordinary privileges. The British received precedence for their diplomatic representative over all others, control over key areas of the country including the Ogaden and a border region known as the Reserved Area, and significant influence over the nation's finances and judiciary. British officers were to command and train the new Ethiopian army. The agreement effectively turned Ethiopia into a temporary British protectorate. It was, however, a necessary compromise. The Emperor needed British financial aid to run his government and British military support to demobilize the unruly Patriot armies and re-establish central control.

The Emperor's second major challenge was internal. The very men who had kept resistance alive, the *Arbegnoch*, were now a threat to the centralized state he sought to rebuild. These Patriot leaders had spent years operating as independent warlords, commanding personal armies and ruling their own territories. They had earned the respect of their people and were not eager to surrender their hard-won autonomy to a distant government in Addis Ababa. The Emperor handled this dilemma with a characteristic mix of reward and ruthlessness.

Loyal and compliant Patriot leaders were brought into the new power structure, granted titles, land, and positions in the provincial administration. Figures like Ras Abebe Aregai, the great resistance leader of Shewa, were made ministers and governors, their power co-opted and institutionalized. Those who defied the Emperor's authority, however, were dealt with mercilessly. The most famous case was that of Belay Zeleke, a charismatic guerrilla leader from Gojjam of humble origins who had become a living legend. He refused to submit to the newly appointed governor of the province, and in 1942 he rose in open rebellion. The uprising was crushed by the new British-trained army. Belay Zeleke was captured, tried for treason, and, in a stark message to other potential rebels, was publicly hanged in Addis Ababa in 1945.

A more serious challenge to the restored imperial order erupted in Tigray in 1943. The "Woyane Rebellion," as it came to be known, was a large-scale peasant uprising fueled by a combination of grievances. The proud Tigrayan nobility felt marginalized by the Shewan-dominated government in Addis Ababa. The peasantry, meanwhile, was enraged by the imposition of new, centrally collected taxes, which they saw as exploitative and corrupt. The rebellion was a direct challenge to the Emperor's modernizing and centralizing agenda. For several months, the rebels controlled most of eastern and southern Tigray, capturing the provincial capital of Mekelle. Haile Selassie's response was swift and devastating. He requested and received assistance from the British Royal Air Force (RAF). In October 1943, British Blenheim bombers flew sorties over Mekelle, bombing the marketplace and the rebels' headquarters. The aerial bombardment broke the back of the rebellion. The psychological shock of seeing their own government use foreign air power against them, combined with the ground assault by the regular army, was too much for the rebel forces, who quickly dispersed. The Woyane rebellion was crushed, but it left a legacy of deep bitterness in Tigray that would smolder for decades.

With his internal authority slowly but surely re-established, the Emperor focused on removing the last vestiges of British control. He was a master of the diplomatic long game. As the Second World War drew to a close, Britain's global power was waning, while a new giant, the United States, was emerging on the world stage. Haile Selassie skillfully played these shifting dynamics to his advantage. In 1944, he successfully negotiated a new Anglo-Ethiopian Agreement, which superseded the 1942 treaty. This new pact restored full sovereignty to Ethiopia. The British relinquished their control over the country's finances, courts, and communications. Most of the British troops were withdrawn, though they controversially retained control over the Ogaden region for several more years, citing the need to manage cross-border Somali disputes.

The Emperor now sought a new, more powerful international patron, and he found one in the United States. The Cold War was beginning to cast its long shadow, and Ethiopia's strategic location in the Horn of Africa, commanding the approaches to the Red Sea, made it a valuable piece of real estate in the global struggle against Communism. Haile Selassie presented himself to Washington as a staunch anti-Communist ally, a reliable Christian monarch in a volatile region. This alignment would become the cornerstone of his foreign policy for the next thirty years. The relationship was cemented by American interests in a large radio communications facility that had been built by the Italians near Asmara in Eritrea.

This facility, which became known as Kagnew Station, was a vital link in the United States' global intelligence and communications network. Securing long-term access to Kagnew Station became a primary objective of American foreign policy in the region.

This American interest in Eritrea dovetailed perfectly with the Emperor's single most important post-war diplomatic objective: the recovery of the former Italian colony. Since the Italian defeat in 1941, Eritrea had been under British Military Administration. Its final political status was undecided. For Haile Selassie, the issue was non-negotiable. He launched an intense, relentless international campaign for the "return" of Eritrea to its "Motherland." The imperial government's argument was threefold. First, they argued on historical and cultural grounds that Eritrea, particularly the highland plateau, was an integral part of historic Ethiopia, the cradle of the Aksumite Empire, that had been unnaturally severed by Italian colonialism. Second, they made a powerful economic case, arguing that landlocked Ethiopia was being strangled without its natural access to the sea through the ports of Massawa and Assab. Third, they appealed to the shared sacrifice of the war, arguing that Ethiopia, as the first victim of fascism, deserved to be made whole.

Within Eritrea itself, the British administration had allowed a new and vibrant political life to flourish. Several political parties emerged, representing a wide spectrum of opinion. The largest and best-organized was the Unionist Party. Led by figures like Tedla Bairu and lavishly funded by the Ethiopian government, it campaigned vigorously for an unconditional union with Ethiopia, echoing the "Motherland" argument. Opposing them was a coalition of parties known as the Independence Bloc. This group, which included the Muslim League and the Liberal Progressive Party, drew its support from the Muslim lowlands and from Eritreans who feared that union with the autocratic and Amhara-dominated Ethiopian empire would mean the end of their more democratic and developed society. A smaller pro-Italy party, representing the interests of the significant Italian settler community, also campaigned for a return to some form of Italian trusteeship.

The fate of Eritrea was initially placed in the hands of the Four-Power Commission, composed of the main Allied victors: the United States, the Soviet Union, Britain, and France. They dispatched a commission of inquiry to Eritrea in 1947 but failed to reach an agreement, their deliberations deadlocked by their own competing Cold War interests. The question was then passed to the newly formed United Nations General Assembly in 1949. The UN sent its own five-nation Commission of Enquiry to Eritrea in 1950 to ascertain the wishes of the population and propose a solution.

The UN Commission found a deeply divided society. They traveled throughout the territory, holding public meetings and accepting petitions. The Unionists organized massive, well-orchestrated demonstrations calling for unity with Ethiopia. The Independence Bloc countered with their own rallies, demanding a sovereign Eritrean state. The Commission's final report reflected these divisions. The delegates from Burma and South Africa recommended a federation, while the delegate from Norway argued for full union. The delegates from Guatemala and Pakistan, swayed by the arguments of the Independence Bloc, recommended a ten-year UN trusteeship leading to full independence.

The final decision was made not in the dusty towns of Eritrea, but in the corridors of power at the UN headquarters at Lake Success, New York. Here, Ethiopia's diplomatic efforts, heavily backed by the United States, proved decisive. The American delegation, eager to secure its strategic interests at Kagnew Station and to reward its new anti-Communist ally, threw its considerable weight behind a compromise that would satisfy Ethiopia's core demands. On December 2, 1950, the UN General Assembly adopted Resolution 390A(V). It rejected both full independence and full union. Instead, it called for a federation.

The resolution was a complex legal creation. It stated that Eritrea would "constitute an autonomous unit federated with Ethiopia under the sovereignty of the Ethiopian Crown." Eritrea was to have its own constitution, its own elected parliament (the Eritrean Assembly), and its own government with authority over all domestic affairs, including its own police force, budget, and official languages (Tigrinya and Arabic). The federal government, which was effectively the Ethiopian government, would have jurisdiction over defense, foreign affairs, currency, and ports. An Imperial Federal Council, with equal numbers of Ethiopian and Eritrean representatives, would advise the Emperor. A UN Commissioner, Eduardo Anze Matienzo of Bolivia, was appointed to oversee the drafting of the Eritrean constitution and the transition to this new federal arrangement.

For the next two years, the process unfolded. The Eritrean constitution, a remarkably democratic document for the region at the time, was drafted and adopted by a representative assembly elected by the Eritrean people in 1952. In March of that year, Eritreans went to the polls to elect their first 68-member Assembly. The Unionist Party won a majority of the seats, and its leader, Tedla Bairu, became the first Chief Executive of Eritrea. On September 11, 1952, Emperor Haile Selassie formally ratified the Eritrean constitution and the Federal Act. The British Military Administration was dissolved, and the Ethiopian flag was raised over the governor's palace in Asmara.

To the world, the solution seemed an elegant and just compromise, one that respected Eritrean autonomy while satisfying Ethiopia's need for sea access. The Emperor hailed it as a great victory, the peaceful reunification of a family long divided. But beneath the surface, the federal arrangement was built on a fundamental and ultimately fatal contradiction. It attempted to yoke a quasi-parliamentary democracy in Eritrea to an absolute monarchy in Ethiopia. For the Eritrean political parties who had fought for independence, the federation was a bitter consolation prize. For Haile Selassie, an emperor whose entire career had been dedicated to the principle of unwavering centralization, the notion of a truly autonomous region within his empire was anathema. The federation was not, in his eyes, a permanent solution, but a temporary and tactical step on the road to a final, complete, and indivisible union.

CHAPTER EIGHTEEN: The Twilight of the Monarchy: Social Unrest and Famine

The Ethiopia that emerged into the second half of the twentieth century presented a study in contradictions. On the world stage, Emperor Haile Selassie had cultivated an image of immense prestige and historical grandeur. He was the elder statesman of Africa, a living symbol of anti-fascist resistance, the host and principal architect of the Organization of African Unity (OAU), which established its permanent headquarters in his capital, Addis Ababa, in 1963. Visiting heads of state were treated to lavish banquets in his Grand Palace, where they were served by waiters in immaculate white gloves and guarded by the emperor's pet lions. To the outside world, Ethiopia was a beacon of African independence, an ancient Christian kingdom ruled by a wise and progressive monarch.

At home, the reality was starkly different. The Emperor's power, meticulously consolidated over decades, was absolute. The Revised Constitution of 1955, promulgated to mark the twenty-fifth anniversary of his coronation, was a masterpiece of autocratic legalism. While it introduced universal adult suffrage and created a popularly elected Chamber of Deputies, these were cosmetic gestures. The document enshrined the Emperor's "divine" right to rule and concentrated all executive, legislative, and judicial power in his hands. The parliament could debate, but it could not legislate without his approval. Ministers served at his pleasure, and the landed aristocracy and the Orthodox Church were bound to him in a web of patronage. Ethiopia was not a modernizing nation-state in the conventional sense; it was a deeply feudal empire where all lines of authority and loyalty led to the person of the Emperor.

For the vast majority of the population, life had changed little in centuries. The peasant farmers who made up nearly ninety percent of the population were trapped in a stifling system of tenancy. In the southern provinces, the legacy of Menelik's conquests had left most of the land in the hands of absentee landlords from the north, to whom the local farmers, the *gabbars*, owed crippling rents, taxes, and labor services that could amount to three-quarters of their total produce. The promised modernization was visible only in patches in the capital and a few other towns. For the rural masses, the government was a distant, extractive force, personified by the tax collector and the local governor.

The first serious crack in this carefully constructed edifice of imperial authority appeared not from the oppressed peasantry, but from within the very heart of the Emperor's modernizing project. On December 13, 1960, while Haile Selassie was on a state visit to Brazil, the tranquil facade of his rule was shattered. A meticulously planned coup d'état was launched by the men he trusted most. The leaders were an unlikely pair of brothers. The intellectual force was Germame Neway, a highly educated provincial governor with a master's degree from Columbia University. Germame was a fervent modernizer, deeply frustrated by the glacial pace of reform and the corruption he saw as endemic to the imperial system. His brother, Brigadier General Mengistu Neway, provided the muscle. He was the commander of the elite Imperial Bodyguard, the *Kebur Zabagna*, the best-trained and best-equipped unit in the entire armed forces.

The plotters moved with speed and precision. The Imperial Bodyguard seized control of the capital, surrounding the key ministries and communication centers. They took dozens of the most powerful figures of the old regime hostage, herding them into the Green Salon of the Guenete Leul Palace. They then went to the residence of the Crown Prince, Asfaw Wossen, a politically timid figure who had long been overshadowed by his father. Under duress, the Crown Prince went on the radio and read a statement prepared by the coup leaders. He announced the formation of a new government that would address the poverty and backwardness of the nation and operate under a constitutional monarchy. It was a direct assault on the Emperor's absolute power. Germame Neway spoke next, delivering a fiery address in which he denounced the old government for enriching itself while the people starved and promised a new era of progress and social justice.

The coup leaders' message resonated strongly with the students at Haile Selassie University, who poured into the streets in support of the promised reforms. But beyond the campus and a few intellectual circles, the rebellion failed to ignite. The plotters had miscalculated the deep-seated, almost religious reverence that much of the population, particularly the peasantry, still held for the Emperor. More decisively, they had failed to secure the support of the two other pillars of the armed forces: the regular army and the air force. These forces, commanded by generals fiercely loyal to the Emperor, saw the Imperial Bodyguard's action not as a progressive revolution but as an act of treason.

From his temporary headquarters in Asmara, the Emperor broadcast a defiant message to the nation, condemning the rebels and calling on the army to crush them. The loyalist forces, led by General Merid Mengesha, began their counter-attack. A fierce battle for control of Addis Ababa erupted. As it became clear that their coup was failing, the rebels grew desperate. In a final, bloody act, they machine-gunned their high-profile hostages in the Green Salon, murdering fifteen of the most powerful men in the empire. The massacre sealed their fate. By December 17, the regular army had regained control of the capital. Germame Neway, cornered and wounded, took his own life. His brother, Mengistu, was captured, put on trial, and publicly hanged a few months later.

The 1960 coup attempt was a failure, but it was a watershed moment. It shattered the myth of an ancient, unchanging empire united in its devotion to the Emperor. It demonstrated for the first time that a modern, educated, and politically conscious opposition existed and was willing to use violence to achieve its aims. The coup's intellectual legacy was profound. The questions the Neway brothers had raised—about land reform, social inequality, and the nature of political power—could no longer be ignored. For the newly politicized generation of university students, the coup plotters were not traitors but martyrs, and their failed rebellion became the foundational event for a decade of growing radicalism.

Throughout the 1960s and into the early 1970s, the main campus of Haile Selassie University, Siddist Kilo, became the epicenter of dissent. Students, inspired by Marxist-Leninist ideology, the global anti-war movement, and other African liberation struggles, grew increasingly bold in their criticism of the regime. Their clandestine newspapers and pamphlets moved beyond calls for reform to outright demands for revolution. Their signature slogan, which they chanted at their frequent and increasingly violent street demonstrations, was *Meret la rashu*—"Land to the Tiller." It was a simple, powerful demand that struck at the very heart of the feudal land tenure system that underpinned the entire imperial order. In 1969, a student leader named Wallelign Mekonnen published a seminal and highly controversial article, "On the Question of Nationalities in Ethiopia," which argued that Ethiopia was not a unified nation-state but an empire of conquered peoples, and that the right of self-determination should be extended to all its ethnic groups. This was a direct challenge to the official narrative of a homogenous, unified Christian nation. The government's response was a predictable cycle of repression: student leaders were arrested, the university was periodically closed, and demonstrations were broken up by the police with tear gas and batons.

While the students were challenging the regime with ideas, a more tangible military threat was growing in the north. The Emperor's dream of reuniting Eritrea with its "Motherland" was turning into a nightmare. The federal arrangement, which had promised Eritrea significant autonomy, had been systematically dismantled. The Emperor and his loyalist Eritrean allies had squeezed the life out of Eritrea's democratic institutions. Political parties and trade unions were banned, freedom of the press was suppressed, and the use of the Tigrinya and Arabic languages in schools and government was curtailed in favor of Amharic. The final act came in November 1962. The Eritrean Assembly, under intense pressure and bribery from Addis Ababa, voted to dissolve itself and to accept the full and unconditional union of Eritrea with Ethiopia. The federation was dead. Eritrea became the empire's fourteenth province.

This forcible annexation was the spark that ignited a full-blown war of national liberation. In 1961, a small group of Muslim

Eritreans in exile had formed the Eritrean Liberation Front (ELF) and launched an armed struggle. The first shot was fired by Hamid Idris Awate on September 1, 1961. After the annexation, the insurgency, which had been a low-level affair, gained widespread support from both Muslims and highland Christians who felt betrayed by the Emperor. Over the next decade, the conflict grew into a protracted and brutal guerrilla war. The Ethiopian army, trained and supplied by the United States, became bogged down in a costly counter-insurgency campaign that it could not win. The Eritrean war became a constant drain on the imperial treasury and a source of growing discontent within the military.

By the early 1970s, the foundations of the ancient regime were visibly crumbling. The international prestige of the Emperor could no longer mask the deep-seated problems at home. Galloping inflation, exacerbated by the global oil crisis of 1973, hit the urban population hard. A severe drought was taking hold in the countryside. Within the armed forces, which had been the bedrock of the Emperor's power, dissent was festering. Junior officers and non-commissioned officers, many of whom were educated and exposed to the radical ideas of the student movement, were growing resentful of a corrupt and incompetent high command drawn from the ranks of the aristocracy. They were tired of fighting and dying in Eritrea for a cause many of them no longer believed in, all while their own pay and conditions remained abysmal. A series of small-scale mutinies over pay and supplies began to break out in remote garrisons in early 1974, seemingly minor events that were actually the first tremors of a massive earthquake.

The final, fatal blow to the monarchy's legitimacy came not from a political manifesto or a military mutiny, but from a catastrophic natural disaster and the government's criminal negligence in response to it. A devastating drought, which had begun in 1972, had by 1973 created a full-blown famine in the northeastern province of Wollo. Hundreds of thousands of peasants were starving to death. Yet the imperial government did everything in its power to conceal the catastrophe. The Emperor was preparing to celebrate his eightieth birthday, and the OAU was holding its tenth anniversary summit in Addis Ababa. News of a massive famine would tarnish the carefully crafted image of a stable and prosperous nation. Provincial officials who tried to sound the alarm were silenced.

The truth, however, could not be hidden forever. In October 1973, a British television journalist, Jonathan Dimbleby, smuggled his crew into Wollo and filmed the horrifying reality of the famine. His documentary, broadcast to a shocked international audience under the title *The Unknown Famine*, showed haunting images of emaciated children and dying peasants. The film was interspersed with clips from the Emperor's lavish birthday celebrations in the capital, creating a devastating and unforgettable portrait of a regime's callous indifference to the suffering of its own people. When the film was eventually shown to students at the university in Addis Ababa, their simmering anger boiled over into uncontrollable rage.

The Wollo famine exposed the imperial system as morally bankrupt, corrupt, and terminally incompetent. It shattered the last vestiges of the Emperor's sacred mystique. The potent combination of urban unrest over inflation, simmering rebellion in the military, a long-running war in Eritrea, and the moral outrage over the hidden famine created a perfect storm. The twilight of the monarchy was over. Night was about to fall.

CHAPTER NINETEEN: The 1974 Revolution and the Rise of the Derg

The ancient imperial edifice, which had stood for centuries, did not fall in a single, mighty crash. It crumbled over a period of nine chaotic months, beginning not with a revolutionary masterplan, but with a series of seemingly minor and disconnected mutinies over pay and conditions in the far-flung garrisons of the Ethiopian army. The first tremor came in January 1974 from a remote outpost at Negelle Borana in the south. Soldiers of the 4th Brigade, living in squalid conditions with a contaminated water supply, detained their commanding officer and sent a list of grievances to the capital. They were not demanding revolution; they were demanding potable water. The Emperor, in a gesture that would prove fatally inadequate, sent a delegation with promises and back-pay, temporarily defusing the situation.

But the spark had been lit. In February, the unrest spread to the Second Division in Asmara, the nerve center of the costly and demoralizing war in Eritrea. Then, on February 10th, non-commissioned officers at the Debre Zeit air force base, just fifty kilometers from the capital, mutinied, holding their own officers hostage and issuing a list of twenty-five demands. Crucially, their demands went beyond simple matters of pay and conditions; they called for the resignation of the Emperor's entire cabinet. The contagion was spreading from the periphery to the very heart of the military establishment.

This wave of military insubordination coincided with, and in turn emboldened, a massive surge of civilian unrest in Addis Ababa. The city was a tinderbox of social and economic grievances. The global oil crisis had sent fuel prices soaring, and the government's decision to raise the price of gasoline by fifty percent was the final straw. On February 18th, the city's taxi drivers went on strike, paralyzing public transport. They were soon joined by teachers, who were protesting a proposed educational reform known as the Sector Review, which they argued would limit educational opportunities for the rural poor. Students from Haile Selassie University, long the vanguard of radical opposition, poured into the streets, clashing with police and chanting their revolutionary slogan, "Land to the Tiller." The capital descended into a state of near-anarchy. On February 23rd, the powerful Confederation of Ethiopian Labour Unions (CELU) called for a general strike, adding the organized working class to the chorus of dissent.

Faced with a mutinous army and a rebellious capital, the government of Prime Minister Aklilu Habte-Wold, a bastion of the old aristocratic order, was paralyzed. On February 27, 1974, after days of rioting and chaos, the entire cabinet resigned. The Emperor, hoping to appease the public and reassert control, accepted their resignation and appointed a new Prime Minister, Lij Endelkachew Makonnen. Endelkachew was a blue-blooded aristocrat but was seen as a liberal reformer. He promised a new constitution that would make the Prime Minister accountable to parliament and pledged to investigate corruption. It was a classic case of too little, too late. The forces that had been unleashed could no longer be contained by promises of gradual reform from a member of the old elite. Power was not being contested in the halls of parliament; it was being redefined in the barracks and on the streets.

Amid the chaos, a new and shadowy organization began to coalesce within the armed forces. It was a response to the breakdown of the military chain of command. With senior officers discredited and junior officers leading mutinies, a mechanism was needed to coordinate the actions of the various disparate military units. In late February, a group of enlisted men in the Second Division in Asmara formed a coordinating committee. The idea spread rapidly. By April, representatives from some forty units of the armed forces, police, and territorial army had gathered in Addis Ababa. They formed a new body, the Coordinating Committee of the Armed Forces, Police, and Territorial Army. This committee, a sprawling and initially anonymous collective of junior officers, NCOs, and privates, would become known to the world by its Amharic name: the Derg.

The Derg was not, at its inception, a revolutionary junta with a clear ideology or a plan to seize power. It was an ad hoc committee born of military necessity, its primary goal to restore order within the army and to ensure that the military's corporate interests were represented in the new political landscape. Its members were mostly majors, captains, and lieutenants, men who were educated and deeply patriotic but who came from humble backgrounds and held a deep-seated resentment for the corrupt, aristocratic high command. The committee operated in secrecy, its decisions made collectively and its public statements issued anonymously. This facelessness was one of its greatest strengths; there was no single leader to be arrested or co-opted. A young, ambitious, and little-known major from the 3rd Division in Harar, Mengistu Haile Mariam, was elected chairman of the committee, but in these early days, he was just one voice among many.

The new Prime Minister, Endelkachew Makonnen, initially saw the Derg as a useful, if unruly, partner. He believed he could use the committee to pressure the old guard into accepting his reforms. It was a fatal miscalculation. The Derg had no interest in propping up a reformed version of the old regime. Over the next few months, it executed a brilliant and methodical "creeping coup." Instead of a single, violent seizure of power, the Derg patiently and systematically dismantled the imperial state piece by piece, all the while proclaiming its loyalty to the Emperor. Their slogan, broadcast constantly on the state-controlled radio they now commanded, was *Ethiopia Tikdem*—"Ethiopia First." It was a vague but potent nationalist motto that masked their true intentions and rallied popular support.

The first targets were the pillars of the old government. In April, the Derg demanded and secured the arrest of the former ministers of the Aklilu cabinet, along with dozens of senior military officials and provincial governors. They were charged with corruption and, most damningly, with concealing the Wollo famine. The Derg had found its moral cause. It presented itself as an instrument of justice, the avenger of the people against a callous and criminal elite. Prime Minister Endelkachew, trying to maintain his authority, was forced to acquiesce to their demands. His government was being hollowed out from within, his power draining away with each new arrest.

Throughout June and July, the Derg's campaign of arrests accelerated. They moved against the most powerful figures in the empire, the men who had been the bedrock of the Emperor's rule. Ras Asrate Kassa, the head of the Crown Council; Ras Mesfin Sileshi, a powerful landowner and conservative stalwart; and members of the Emperor's own Imperial Court were rounded up and imprisoned. The Emperor, increasingly isolated in his Jubilee Palace, was powerless to stop them. He was becoming a prisoner in his own home, his authority evaporating as the men who had sustained it were led away one by one. By the end of July, Endelkachew Makonnen's brief and ineffectual tenure as Prime Minister was over. He too was arrested, and the Derg appointed a new, more pliable civilian Prime Minister, Mikael Imru.

Having decapitated the old regime, the Derg turned its attention to destroying the very institution of the monarchy. It launched a ferocious propaganda campaign against the Emperor himself. The carefully cultivated image of a benevolent, god-like father of the nation was systematically shredded. State television repeatedly broadcast Jonathan Dimbleby's harrowing documentary, *The Unknown Famine*, often intercutting its scenes of starvation with footage of lavish imperial banquets and the Emperor feeding choice cuts of meat to his pet dogs. The committee released detailed reports on the Emperor's vast personal fortune, held in secret Swiss bank accounts, contrasting it with the abject poverty of his subjects. The mystique that had surrounded Haile Selassie for half a century was methodically dissolved in a bath of television images and radio broadcasts. The god-king was revealed to be a mere mortal, a frail, elderly man who had presided over a system of unimaginable cruelty and neglect.

By late August, the stage was set for the final act. The Derg had consolidated its control over the military, decapitated the aristocracy, and destroyed the Emperor's popular legitimacy. It moved to strip him of his last formal powers. On August 15, the Imperial Guard, the Emperor's Praetorian Guard and the force that had attempted the 1960 coup, was disbanded and its members dispersed to remote posts. The Imperial Court was dissolved, and the Jubilee Palace was nationalized as property of the Ethiopian people. The Crown Council was abolished. Every institutional pillar of the monarchy had been kicked away.

The end came on the morning of September 12, 1974. The date was deliberately chosen. It was the second day of the Ethiopian New Year, a time of celebration, but it was also the day before the Feast of the Finding of the True Cross, or Meskel, one of the most important religious holidays in the country, a day on which the Emperor had traditionally presided over a great national bonfire. By acting on this day, the Derg ensured that the capital would be quiet and that there would be no public ceremony to rally loyalist sentiment.

A small delegation of Derg officers, led by Major Debela Dinsa, drove to the Jubilee Palace in a convoy that included a humble, olive-green Volkswagen Beetle. They were met by the 82-year-old Emperor, dressed in a formal suit, a small, dignified figure in the vast emptiness of his now-powerless court. Major Debela read a proclamation, broadcast live on the radio. It accused Haile Selassie of abusing his authority, of enriching himself at the expense of his people, and of presiding over a system of injustice. It declared that, in the name of the Ethiopian people and the armed forces, he was deposed.

The Emperor listened in silence. According to eyewitness accounts, he made no protest, simply stating that if the revolution was for the good of the country, he would accept his fate. He was then escorted out of the palace, past the bowing retainers who were seeing him for the last time. He was not placed in a limousine, but in the back of the small Volkswagen, a final, calculated humiliation. As the car drove away, taking the last Emperor of the Solomonic dynasty to an undisclosed place of imprisonment, it was forced to stop to allow a flock of sheep to cross the road. The 3,000-year-old monarchy, which traced its origins to King Solomon and the Queen of Sheba, ended not with a bang, but with a quiet, almost surreal whimper.

That afternoon, the Derg formally announced that it had assumed full state power. It declared the establishment of a Provisional Military Administrative Council (PMAC) to govern the country. The constitution was suspended, and parliament was dissolved. In a final, curious gesture, the Derg proclaimed that the Crown Prince, Asfaw Wossen, who was abroad receiving medical treatment, would be "King-designate" upon his return, but not Emperor, and that his powers would be ceremonial. It was a transparent fiction; the monarchy was dead, and the Crown Prince, who wisely chose to remain in exile, would never take the throne. Real power now lay with the anonymous committee of soldiers.

The Ethiopian revolution had been, up to this point, almost completely bloodless. It was a testament to the Derg's strategic patience and the utter collapse of the old regime's will to fight. But the committee that now held the destiny of the nation in its hands was far from a unified body. It was a coalition of over one hundred officers and NCOs, encompassing a wide spectrum of political views, from moderate nationalists to committed Marxist-Leninists. With their common enemy, the Emperor, now gone, the deep ideological fissures within the Derg were about to erupt. The initial phase of the revolution, the "creeping coup," was over. A new and far more violent phase, a struggle for the soul of the revolution itself, was about to begin.

CHAPTER TWENTY: The Red Terror and the Ethiopian Civil War

The quiet, almost anticlimactic, removal of Emperor Haile Selassie in September 1974 did not usher in the era of unity and progress promised by the Derg's vague slogan, *Ethiopia Tikdem*. Instead, it ripped the lid off a cauldron of competing ambitions and ideologies. The revolution had succeeded in decapitating the old regime, but it had no clear idea of what to build in its place. The Derg itself, a sprawling and anonymous committee of over one hundred soldiers, was a microcosm of this confusion, a volatile mix of junior officers, NCOs, and privates who ranged from moderate nationalists to fervent, radical Marxists. With their common enemy gone, they turned on each other in a brutal struggle for the soul of the revolution. The bloodless coup was over; a new and terrifyingly violent chapter was about to begin.

The first chairman of the Derg was a popular and respected Eritrean general, Aman Andom. He was a moderate nationalist who envisioned a peaceful, political solution to the long-running war in his home province of Eritrea and a gradual transition to a civilian-led government. This put him on a direct collision course with the committee's increasingly powerful radical faction, a group centered on a hardline and ambitious major named Mengistu Haile Mariam. Mengistu and his allies saw Aman's conciliatory approach as a betrayal of the revolution. They demanded a military solution in Eritrea and a swift, ruthless purge of the old imperial elite. The power struggle came to a head in November 1974. After refusing to sign orders for a new offensive in Eritrea and the execution of high-ranking political prisoners, General Aman was placed under house arrest. On the evening of November 23, he was killed in a firefight while resisting arrest at his home.

That same night, the revolution took its definitive and bloody turn. On the orders of the radical faction now in control of the Derg, sixty of the most senior officials of the former imperial government were summarily executed without trial in the cellars of the Akaki prison. The victims included two former prime ministers, sixteen generals, and Ras Asrate Kassa, the grandson of a former emperor and a leading figure of the old aristocracy. The "Saturday Massacre," as it became known, was a calculated act of terror. It was a signal that there would be no compromise, no reconciliation with the past. It permanently slammed the door on any possibility of a moderate, negotiated transition. The radicals, with Mengistu as their rising star, were now in command, and their instrument of rule would be the gun.

Having eliminated the "enemies of the past," the Derg now turned to remaking the nation's economic and social foundations. Inspired by the socialist doctrines that were animating their most influential members, they embarked on a program of revolutionary transformation from above. On March 4, 1975, they issued their most sweeping and consequential decree: Proclamation No. 31, the Public Ownership of Rural Lands Proclamation. With the stroke of a pen, it abolished the private ownership of all rural land in Ethiopia. The proclamation declared that all land was now the collective property of the Ethiopian people. The ancient, oppressive system of tenancy, which had kept millions of peasants in a state of near-serfdom, was annihilated overnight. The revolutionary slogan of the student movement, "Land to the Tiller," had become law.

The proclamation was wildly popular among the rural masses, who were organized into Peasant Associations to administer the newly collectivized land. It was a genuine social revolution that destroyed the economic basis of the old feudal aristocracy. This was swiftly followed by the nationalization of all urban land and extra rental houses, and the seizure of banks, insurance companies, and major industrial enterprises. In a matter of months, the Derg had obliterated the old economic order and established a centrally planned, socialist state.

The very student radicals and leftist intellectuals who had for years called for such a revolution, however, were horrified. They had dreamed of a popular revolution that would lead to a civilian-led "people's government," not the replacement of one form of autocracy with another. The Derg, they argued, was a military junta that had "hijacked" their revolution. This opposition coalesced around two main civilian Marxist-Leninist parties. The most formidable was the Ethiopian People's Revolutionary Party (EPRP). Composed largely of students and intellectuals who had returned from exile, the EPRP demanded an immediate end to military rule and the formation of a provisional civilian government. They had a large, clandestine urban network and began to view the Derg as a fascist junta that had to be overthrown by force.

A rival group, the All-Ethiopia Socialist Movement (MEISON), took a different strategic path. Led by the intellectual Haile Fida, MEISON argued for a strategy of "critical support" for the Derg. They believed that the military committee was politically unsophisticated and could be guided from within. By collaborating with the Derg, they hoped to steer the revolution towards their own brand of socialism and eventually ease the soldiers out of power. This ideological split between the two main leftist parties would prove to be a fatal one, creating a toxic atmosphere of paranoia and rivalry that the Derg would ruthlessly exploit.

By 1976, the verbal sparring had escalated into open warfare. The EPRP launched a campaign of urban guerrilla warfare, assassinating Derg officials, members of MEISON, and other government supporters. Addis Ababa became a battleground, a city of fear where assassinations and retaliatory killings were a daily occurrence. Mengistu Haile Mariam, who by this point had consolidated his power within the Derg—a process that involved a bloody shootout in February 1977 in which his main rival, the then-chairman Tafari Benti, and several other Derg members were killed—decided to crush the EPRP once and for all.

On April 17, 1977, standing before a vast crowd in Addis Ababa's Revolution Square, Mengistu held up three bottles filled with a red liquid symbolizing the blood of imperialists, feudalists, and the EPRP. He smashed the bottles to the ground and roared, "Death to counter-revolutionaries! Death to the EPRP!" This was the official declaration of the *Qey Shibir*, or Red Terror. What followed was a state-orchestrated campaign of carnage that plunged the capital and other towns into a nightmare of unimaginable brutality.

The main instruments of the Red Terror were the newly empowered neighborhood associations, or *kebeles*. These local committees, initially formed to administer nationalized housing, were now armed and given carte blanche to root out and eliminate suspected "counter-revolutionaries." Every neighborhood had its own *kebele* security squad, which set up roadblocks, conducted house-to-house searches, and operated its own prisons. With MEISON cadres providing the ideological justification and often pointing out the targets, the *kebeles* unleashed a wave of arrests, torture, and summary executions.

The primary targets were the youth. High school and university students, suspected of being EPRP members or sympathizers, were dragged from their homes at night. Their bodies were often dumped on the streets the next morning with placards pinned to them, denouncing them as enemies of the revolution. This was a deliberate tactic to terrorize the population into submission. In one of the most ghoulish practices of the era, families of the victims were often forced to pay the *kebele* for the cost of the bullet used to kill their child before they were allowed to retrieve the body for burial. The terror was not just about eliminating an organized political opposition; it was about atomizing society, destroying any potential for dissent by creating an atmosphere of pervasive, paralyzing fear. Thousands, perhaps tens of thousands, were killed in Addis Ababa alone.

Having used MEISON to help destroy the EPRP, Mengistu then turned on his erstwhile allies. By mid-1977, MEISON's leaders realized that they had no real influence over the Derg and that their dream of steering the revolution had been a fatal illusion. When they attempted to break away, Mengistu hunted them down with the same ferocity he had shown the EPRP. Most of MEISON's leadership, including Haile Fida, were arrested and subsequently executed. By 1978, the urban leftist opposition, both EPRP and MEISON, had been physically annihilated. The Red Terror had succeeded. Mengistu Haile Mariam was the undisputed, absolute ruler of Ethiopia.

While this brutal urban war was raging, the country was also being torn apart by a full-scale international conflict and a series of escalating regional wars. The chaos in Addis Ababa had not gone unnoticed by Ethiopia's neighbor and rival, Somalia. The Somali president, Siad Barre, saw a golden opportunity to realize his long-held nationalist dream of a "Greater Somalia" by seizing the vast, Somali-inhabited Ogaden region of eastern Ethiopia. In July 1977, the regular Somali National Army, supported by the Western Somali Liberation Front (WSLF), launched a massive invasion.

The invasion was a spectacular initial success. The Somali army, well-equipped and trained by its long-time patron, the Soviet Union, smashed through the thinly stretched Ethiopian defenses. Within months, they had captured nearly ninety percent of the Ogaden and were threatening the key cities of Harar and Dire Dawa. The Ethiopian revolution seemed on the verge of collapse, attacked from within by the EPRP and from without by the Somali army. It was at this desperate moment that one of the most dramatic geopolitical realignments of the Cold War occurred. The Soviet Union, seeing a more valuable and ideologically aligned prize in the larger, more strategically important Ethiopia, abandoned its long-time client Somalia and threw its full support behind Mengistu's regime.

What followed was a massive and decisive intervention. The USSR orchestrated a gigantic air and sealift of tanks, artillery, and military hardware to Ethiopia. Even more consequentially, some fifteen thousand combat troops from Fidel Castro's Cuba were airlifted to the front lines to fight alongside the beleaguered Ethiopian army. With this new arsenal and the battle-hardened Cuban soldiers leading the counter-attack, the tide turned dramatically. In early 1978, the combined Ethiopian-Cuban force launched a major offensive, routing the Somali army and driving it out of the Ogaden in complete disarray. The victory was a stunning reversal of fortune. It was a catastrophe from which Somalia would never fully recover, but for Mengistu, it was a moment of supreme triumph. He had defended the nation's territorial integrity, solidified his rule, and secured a powerful new superpower patron.

The victory in the Ogaden, however, did not bring peace. It merely allowed the Derg to refocus its new Soviet-supplied military might on the other civil wars that were raging across the country. In the north, the war for Eritrean independence had reached a critical stage. During the chaos of 1977, the two main guerrilla fronts, the Eritrean Liberation Front (ELF) and the more effective, Marxist-led Eritrean People's Liberation Front (EPLF), had made huge gains, capturing almost all of the territory except for the capital, Asmara, and a few other besieged garrisons. After the Ogaden war, the Derg transferred its best divisions and its new Soviet weaponry to the Eritrean front. It launched a series of massive human-wave offensives, most famously the "Red Star Campaign" of 1982, which involved over one hundred thousand soldiers. These campaigns were incredibly brutal and destructive, causing immense suffering to the civilian population, but they failed to dislodge the EPLF, which had tactically retreated to its northern mountain stronghold around the town of Nakfa. The Eritrean war settled into a long, bloody stalemate.

Meanwhile, a new and formidable insurgency was gathering strength in the neighboring province of Tigray. The Tigray People's Liberation Front (TPLF), formed in 1975 by a small group of radical students, had grown into a highly disciplined and effective guerrilla army. It established a strong base of support among the Tigrayan peasantry, who were alienated by the Derg's brutal policies and the legacy of Amhara domination. Throughout the late 1970s and 1980s, the TPLF steadily expanded its control over the Tigrayan countryside, fighting a classic "people's war" against the much larger but less mobile Ethiopian army. In other parts of the country, other ethno-nationalist fronts, such as the Oromo Liberation Front (OLF), were also waging their own insurgencies, though on a smaller scale. By the beginning of the 1980s, Mengistu's regime, having consolidated its power through a campaign of terror, was now the master of a garrison state, mired in a series of intractable and ruinously expensive civil wars that were bleeding the nation dry.

CHAPTER TWENTY-ONE: The Fall of the Derg and the Transitional Government

By the late 1980s, the revolutionary fire that had consumed the Ethiopian monarchy had burned itself out, leaving behind a cold, dark ruin. The regime of Mengistu Haile Mariam, which had promised a new dawn of socialist progress, had delivered only a perpetual night of war, terror, and starvation. The state, renamed the People's Democratic Republic of Ethiopia (PDRE) in 1987 in a cosmetic shift to nominal civilian rule, was a hollow shell. Over sixty percent of the national budget was devoured by a military mired in a series of unwinnable civil wars. The centrally planned economy was a catastrophic failure, incapable of feeding its own people. The vague, hopeful slogan of *Ethiopia Tikdem* had been replaced by the grim reality of a bankrupt and exhausted garrison state.

The final decade of the Derg's rule was bookended by famine. The great famine of 1984-85 was a cataclysm that dwarfed the Wollo famine that had helped topple the Emperor. Horrifying images of skeletal children and desolate landscapes, broadcast to the world, prompted an unprecedented global response, most famously the Live Aid concerts. For Mengistu's government, however, the famine was not just a natural disaster but a political and military opportunity. The regime's primary response was to launch two of the most brutal social engineering projects in modern African history: resettlement and villagization.

The resettlement program aimed to forcibly move up to 1.5 million people from the drought-stricken, rebel-infested northern highlands of Tigray and Wollo to supposedly fertile, unoccupied lands in the south and west. The government presented it as a humane solution to recurrent drought. In practice, it was a campaign of mass abduction, a counter-insurgency strategy designed to drain the sea of popular support in which the rebel fish swam. Families were rounded up at gunpoint, separated from their kin, and herded onto trucks and cargo planes for a journey to a "promised land" that often proved to be unprepared, disease-ridden, and culturally alien. Tens of thousands died in transit or in the squalid, ill-equipped resettlement camps.

The villagization program was even more ambitious. It aimed to completely restructure rural society by moving virtually the entire rural population into new, planned villages. The stated goal was to provide peasants with modern amenities like schools, clinics, and clean water. The real purpose was control. By concentrating the population in centralized villages, the Derg could more easily monitor them, tax them, and, most importantly, conscript their sons into the ever-hungry army. Across the country, millions of peasants were forced to dismantle their ancestral homesteads and rebuild them, often at their own expense, on designated plots of land. These programs caused immense social dislocation and a catastrophic drop in agricultural production, all while failing to crush the insurgencies they were designed to defeat.

The regime's other critical lifeline was also being severed. The Soviet Union, the Derg's superpower patron, was undergoing a profound transformation. Under the leadership of Mikhail Gorbachev, the policies of *glasnost* (openness) and *perestroika* (restructuring) signaled a fundamental shift in Soviet foreign policy. Moscow was no longer willing or able to prop up expensive, inefficient, and brutal client states like Mengistu's Ethiopia. The massive shipments of arms and ammunition that had sustained the Derg's war machine for a decade slowed to a trickle and then stopped. Mengistu was informed in no uncertain terms that he needed to find a political solution to his internal wars. The military crutch he had leaned on for his entire rule was being kicked away.

As the Derg weakened, its enemies grew stronger. The rebel movements in the north had evolved from small guerrilla bands into formidable conventional armies. The Eritrean People's Liberation Front (EPLF) had become one of the most effective fighting forces on the continent. In March 1988, at the Battle of Afabet in northern Eritrea, the EPLF achieved a stunning and decisive victory. In a coordinated, multi-front assault, they overran the headquarters of the Ethiopian army on the Nacfa front, annihilating three entire divisions and capturing vast quantities of tanks, artillery, and equipment. Afabet was the Derg's Dien Bien Phu, a catastrophic military and psychological defeat from which its army in Eritrea would never recover.

A year later, the other major northern front collapsed. The Tigray People's Liberation Front (TPLF), which had spent over a decade building its military strength and political base in the Tigrayan countryside, went on the offensive. In February 1989, TPLF forces routed the Derg army and captured Mekelle, the provincial capital of Tigray. The back of the Ethiopian army in the north had been broken. These victories were not just tactical; they were strategic. The rebels now possessed enough captured heavy weaponry to transform themselves from a guerrilla insurgency into a mechanized force capable of challenging the Derg for control of the entire country. The TPLF, recognizing the need for a broader political front, had already brought together other smaller ethno-nationalist groups to form a coalition known as the Ethiopian People's Revolutionary Democratic Front (EPRDF).

The catastrophic defeats at Afabet and Mekelle sent shockwaves through the Ethiopian military establishment. For years, senior commanders had privately expressed their despair at Mengistu's ruinous military strategy and his refusal to consider a negotiated peace. With the northern armies in full retreat, they decided that the only way to save the country from complete collapse was to remove the dictator. In May 1989, while Mengistu was on a state visit to East Germany, a group of his most senior generals launched a coup d'état. The plot was led by the former chief of staff and the air force commander. They seized the Ministry of Defense and announced that they were taking control to bring an end to the endless civil war.

The coup, however, was poorly planned and failed to secure the support of key units outside the capital. Mengistu, cutting his trip short, flew back to Ethiopia and, with the help of loyalist forces, ruthlessly crushed the rebellion. His revenge was swift and savage. He had a dozen of his most experienced surviving generals executed. This purge, coming on the heels of the recent battlefield disasters, was the final, fatal blow to the morale and command structure of the Ethiopian army. At the very moment it faced its greatest existential threat, the army was rendered leaderless, its most capable commanders either dead or disgraced.

With the Derg's army in disarray, the EPRDF, with the TPLF as its dominant force, began its inexorable push south out of Tigray. The war entered a new and final phase. This was no longer a regional insurgency; it was a conventional military campaign for control of the state. Throughout 1990, EPRDF forces, often in coordination with the EPLF, advanced deep into the Amhara heartlands of Wollo and Gondar, regions that had been the historic bedrock of the Ethiopian state. The Derg's army, composed largely of demoralized and poorly trained conscripts, offered little effective resistance, often abandoning their positions and surrendering by the thousands.

As the military situation deteriorated beyond repair, the international community, particularly the United States, grew increasingly alarmed at the prospect of a chaotic collapse. The recent implosion of the Somali state next door served as a terrifying example of what could happen. Washington, seeing the EPRDF's victory as inevitable, decided to step in to manage the transition. In early 1991, the United States brokered peace talks, scheduled to be held in London at the end of May. It was a conference to negotiate the terms of the Derg's surrender.

By May, the end was near. The EPLF had captured the Eritrean port of Massawa and was tightening its siege of Asmara. The EPRDF, in a multi-pronged offensive codenamed Operation Tewodros, had seized control of most of the country and its forces were now camped on the hills surrounding Addis Ababa. The capital was gripped by a quiet panic. Inside his fortified palace, Mengistu Haile Mariam could hear the approaching thunder. On the morning of May 21, 1991, he gathered the members of his cabinet and, after a rambling final speech, announced that he was leaving to inspect troops in the south. He boarded a plane at the airport and, instead of flying south, ordered the pilot to fly to

Nairobi, Kenya. From there, he was granted asylum by his friend and fellow dictator, Robert Mugabe, in Zimbabwe. The man who had ruled Ethiopia with an iron fist for seventeen years had fled, abandoning his crumbling regime to its fate.

With Mengistu gone, the government in Addis Ababa ceased to function. The acting president, General Tesfaye Gebre Kidan, presided over a state that existed only in name. At the peace conference in London, chaired by the American Assistant Secretary of State for African Affairs, Herman Cohen, the reality on the ground was clear. The Derg's representatives were men with no army and no government. Cohen, communicating by phone with the EPRDF's leader, Meles Zenawi, took a decisive step. Fearing a bloodbath and a total breakdown of order in the capital, he publicly urged the EPRDF to enter Addis Ababa.

On the morning of May 28, 1991, EPRDF tanks and truckloads of young, disciplined guerrilla fighters, many of whom had never seen a city before, rolled into the capital. There was almost no resistance. The seventeen-year reign of terror and war was over. The people of Addis Ababa, uncertain of what this new army from the north would bring, emerged from their homes into a city that was eerily calm.

The task of creating a new political order began immediately. In July 1991, the EPRDF convened a National Conference in Addis Ababa. It was a broad gathering of most of the country's major political and ethnic movements, including the Oromo Liberation Front (OLF). The conference adopted a document that would serve as an interim constitution: the Transitional Charter. It was a radical departure from the hyper-centralized Ethiopian state of both the Emperor and the Derg. The Charter guaranteed fundamental human rights, established a framework for a transitional government, and, most controversially, enshrined in its first article the right of the "nations, nationalities and peoples" of Ethiopia to self-determination, a right which it explicitly defined as including the option of secession.

A new 87-seat Council of Representatives was established to act as a transitional legislature, with seats allocated to the various participating fronts. The EPRDF, as the victor in the war, naturally held a dominant position with 32 seats. Meles Zenawi, the quiet, intellectual leader of the TPLF and chairman of the EPRDF, was elected president of the new Transitional Government of Ethiopia (TGE).

One of the first and most significant acts of the new government was to address the thirty-year-old question of Eritrea. The TPLF and the EPLF had been close military allies in the war against the Derg, united by a shared enemy. As part of their alliance, the TPLF had long ago recognized Eritrea's right to determine its own future. The Transitional Charter now made this official. The TGE formally recognized the right of the Eritrean people to a referendum on independence. The EPLF, which had established its own provisional government in Asmara after its victory, scheduled the referendum for April 1993. The result was a foregone conclusion. An overwhelming 99.8 percent of Eritreans voted for independence. On May 24, 1993, Eritrea became a sovereign nation, and Ethiopia, for the first time in its modern history, was officially a landlocked country. The longest war in Africa had ended in a peaceful and negotiated divorce.

The early days of the TGE were fraught with challenges. The country was awash with hundreds of thousands of demobilized and unemployed soldiers from the Derg's defeated army. The economy had completely collapsed. And the new politics of ethnicity, explicitly encouraged by the Charter, proved to be a volatile force. The alliance with the OLF, one of the largest ethnic groups in the country, quickly soured. Feeling marginalized within the EPRDF-dominated government, the OLF withdrew from the TGE in June 1992 and resumed its armed struggle. It was a clear sign that the road from a centralized, authoritarian empire to a decentralized, democratic federation would be a long and difficult one.

CHAPTER TWENTY-TWO: The Federal Democratic Republic: A New Constitution

The rebel fighters of the Ethiopian People's Revolutionary Democratic Front (EPRDF) who marched into Addis Ababa in May 1991 were not just conquerors; they were architects with a radical blueprint for a new nation. For the first time in its long history, Ethiopia was to be deconstructed and rebuilt not as a unitary empire demanding assimilation, but as a voluntary federation of its constituent peoples. The Transitional Charter adopted in July 1991 was the preliminary sketch, a bold promise of a new beginning. The next four years were dedicated to the monumental task of turning that sketch into a permanent constitution, a process that would formally end the three-thousand-year-old tradition of a centralized, imperial state and inaugurate a new, experimental, and deeply controversial political order.

The Transitional Government of Ethiopia (TGE), with the EPRDF in firm control, set about its work with a sense of revolutionary purpose. The country was stabilized, the massive army of the Derg was demobilized, and a new political discourse, centered on the rights of "nations, nationalities, and peoples," was introduced. This new vocabulary was the core of the EPRDF's ideology, a theory known as ethnic federalism. Forged in the long guerrilla war in the mountains of Tigray, this doctrine held that the Ethiopian empire had been, in essence, a prison of nations, dominated by a ruling Amhara elite who had suppressed the languages, cultures, and identities of the country's other eighty-plus ethnic groups. The only way to prevent the state from disintegrating, the theory went, was to recognize these historic grievances and rebuild the nation on the basis of a voluntary union of equal peoples, each with the right to govern itself.

In 1993, with the Eritrean question settled and a degree of stability achieved, the TGE established a Constitutional Drafting Commission to begin the formal process of creating the new state. The Commission was a large body, tasked with preparing a draft document based on the principles laid out in the Transitional Charter. It held hearings and collected input from various political groups, but there was little doubt that the final product would reflect the ideological vision of the EPRDF. Once a draft was completed, the TGE announced the election of a 547-member Constituent Assembly, a body whose sole purpose would be to debate, amend, and ratify the new constitution.

The elections for this assembly, held in June 1994, provided a clear indication of the political landscape that was taking shape. The EPRDF, a coalition of four ethnically-based parties dominated by the Tigray People's Liberation Front (TPLF), swept the board, winning 484 of the 547 seats. The victory was overwhelming, but it was also uncontested in many areas. Most of the major opposition parties, who had initially participated in the transitional government, had either been marginalized or had chosen to boycott the process. Groups like the Oromo Liberation Front (OLF) and the All Amhara People's Organization (AAPO) argued that the EPRDF was systematically closing the political space, harassing their members, and creating a one-party state under the guise of a multi-party transition. They viewed the constitutional process as a rubber-stamping exercise designed to legitimize EPRDF rule.

Regardless of the boycott, the newly elected Constituent Assembly convened in Addis Ababa. For five months, the delegates debated the draft constitution article by article. While the outcome was never in doubt, the debates were often lively, providing a public forum for the airing of profoundly different visions of the Ethiopian state. The central, and by far the most explosive, issue was the question of self-determination.

The result of these deliberations was the Constitution of the Federal Democratic Republic of Ethiopia, which was formally adopted by the Assembly on December 8, 1994. It was a document unlike any other in the country's history. It established a federal republic with a parliamentary system of government. Power was divided between a central federal government and nine newly created regional states, or *kilils*, which were drawn largely along ethno-linguistic lines. These were Tigray, Afar, Amhara, Oromia, Somali, Benishangul-Gumuz, the Southern Nations, Nationalities, and Peoples' Region (SNNPR), Gambela, and Harari. The capital, Addis Ababa, and later Dire Dawa, were designated as federally administered chartered cities.

The constitution created a bicameral parliament. The lower house, the House of Peoples' Representatives, was the main legislative body, with its 547 members elected by popular vote. The Prime Minister, as the head of government, would be chosen from the party that won a majority in this house. The upper house, the House of the Federation, was a more unusual body. Its members were not directly elected but were chosen by the state councils of the various ethnic groups. Its primary role was to interpret the constitution and, crucially, to arbitrate disputes between the regional states and to oversee the rights of the nations and nationalities. The President was to be a largely ceremonial head of state, elected by a joint session of the two houses.

The document contained a long list of human and democratic rights, guaranteeing freedom of speech, assembly, and religion. It also formally separated state and religion, a significant move in a country where the Orthodox Church had been fused with the monarchy for centuries. The most radical and contested provision, however, was Article 39. This article, titled "Rights of Nations, Nationalities, and Peoples," was the legal cornerstone of the entire ethnic federalist project. It stated, in its first clause, that "Every Nation, Nationality and People in Ethiopia has an unconditional right to self-determination, including the right to secession."

Article 39 was a political earthquake. To its supporters in the EPRDF, it was a "pact of peoples," the ultimate guarantee that no single group would ever again dominate the others. It was a constitutional "escape clause" that made the union voluntary; by guaranteeing the right to leave, it gave every group a reason to stay. To its many critics, however, it was a reckless and dangerous folly. They saw it as a recipe for the eventual disintegration of the state, a constitutional license for secession that would institutionalize ethnic division and undermine the very concept of a common Ethiopian national identity. They argued that it would empower ethnic entrepreneurs and turn every political dispute into a potential question of national sovereignty.

Another fundamental and equally controversial provision of the new constitution was its stance on land. Echoing the 1975 proclamation of the Derg, Article 40 declared that "Land is a common property of the Nations, Nationalities and Peoples of Ethiopia and shall not be subject to sale or other means of exchange." All land, both rural and urban, remained the property of the state. Peasants and pastoralists were granted the right to use their land, but they could not own it, sell it, or mortgage it. The EPRDF argued that this would protect poor farmers from being bought out by wealthy elites and would prevent the re-emergence of the old feudal landlord class. Critics countered that it made every farmer a tenant of the state, created a profound sense of insecurity, and discouraged long-term investment in the land. It also gave the ruling party immense power, as the state's control over this most vital of resources could be used as a tool of political patronage and control.

With the new constitution in place, the final step in the transition was to hold the country's first-ever multi-party national elections. These were scheduled for May 1995. The elections were to choose members for the new federal House of Peoples' Representatives and for the various state councils. Once again, however, the process was marred by the deep rift between the EPRDF and the opposition. Claiming continued harassment and a lack of a level playing field, most of the major opposition parties that had boycotted the 1994 assembly elections also boycotted the 1995 general election. The result was a political landscape almost entirely devoid of a credible national opposition.

The outcome of the May 1995 election was a foregone conclusion. The EPRDF and its affiliated "partner" parties, which it had created to represent ethnic groups not included in its four core movements, won a landslide victory, securing 483 of the 547 seats in the federal parliament. The remaining seats went to a handful of small, independent parties. The election was a watershed moment, the first time in Ethiopian history that a government had been formed through a multi-party electoral process. However, the opposition boycott meant that its democratic legitimacy was immediately called into question, both at home and abroad. Critics argued that Ethiopia had simply traded one form of one-party rule for another, more sophisticated, version.

In August 1995, the transition period officially came to an end. The Federal Democratic Republic of Ethiopia (FDRE) was formally inaugurated. The newly elected parliament convened and put the new constitutional machinery into motion. As the leader of the victorious EPRDF coalition, Meles Zenawi, the man who had been the transitional president for four years, was elected as the country's first Prime Minister, the post that now held the real executive power. In a move designed to reflect the ethnic calculus of the new federation, the parliament elected Dr. Negasso Gidada, an Oromo and a member of the Oromo People's Democratic Organization (OPDO), one of the EPRDF's constituent parties, to the ceremonial post of President.

The new government faced a daunting array of challenges. It had to rebuild a country shattered by decades of war and famine. It had to demobilize tens of thousands of former guerrilla fighters and integrate them into a new national army. It had to liberalize a collapsed state-run economy and attract foreign investment. And it had to manage the complex and often volatile politics of its own federal creation.

The early years of the FDRE were a period of relative optimism and significant change. The new regional states were established, and for the first time, languages like Oromo, Somali, and Tigrinya were used in local government and primary education. A program of economic liberalization, guided by the World Bank and the IMF, began to bear fruit, and the economy started to grow after decades of stagnation. The government embarked on ambitious projects to build roads, schools, and clinics, particularly in the historically neglected rural areas.

Beneath the surface, however, the tensions inherent in the new system were palpable. The EPRDF, born as a secretive and highly disciplined guerrilla front, struggled to transform itself into a genuinely democratic political party. The lines between the party and the state remained deeply blurred. The government's commitment to democratic rights often seemed conditional, and journalists and opposition figures who crossed the line faced harassment and imprisonment. The "question of nationalities," which the EPRDF claimed to have solved, proved to be far from settled. The OLF continued its low-level insurgency in the south, and simmering border disputes between the newly created regional states, particularly between Oromia and the Somali region, periodically flared into violent conflict.

The most critical relationship was with the new nation to the north. In the first few years after Eritrean independence, relations between the two governments, led by the former comrades-in-arms Meles Zenawi and Isaias Afwerki, were exceptionally close. They signed agreements on free trade and the free movement of people, and Eritrea continued to use the Ethiopian currency, the birr. To many, it seemed a model for a post-conflict relationship. But this "honeymoon" period masked deep-seated disagreements over trade, currency, and, most importantly, the precise demarcation of their long and poorly defined common border. The leaders who had fought together as brothers in the war against the Derg would soon find themselves on a collision course, and the new federal republic, born from one long war, was about to be plunged into another, even more destructive, conflict.

CHAPTER TWENTY-THREE: Conflict and Tensions: The Ethio-Eritrean War (1998-2000)

The peaceful, negotiated divorce of Ethiopia and Eritrea in 1993 was celebrated as a model for post-conflict resolution in Africa. The two leaders, Meles Zenawi of Ethiopia and Isaias Afwerki of Eritrea, were former brothers-in-arms, their respective rebel fronts having fought as close allies to overthrow the brutal Derg regime. In the first few years of Eritrean independence, this camaraderie seemed to hold. A spirit of optimism prevailed, and the two nations became deeply intertwined. Agreements were signed guaranteeing the free movement of goods and people across their long, open border. The Eritrean economy, for all practical purposes, was an extension of Ethiopia's; Eritreans conducted business using the Ethiopian currency, the birr, and the Ethiopian port of Assab served as a vital, tariff-free outlet for its landlocked neighbor. It was a relationship so close that many observers spoke not of two separate countries, but of a de facto confederation.

This "honeymoon" period, however, masked a series of growing frictions, rooted in the very different paths the two new states were taking. The relationship between Meles and Isaias, while born of shared struggle, was also one of rivalry between two proud, strong-willed leaders. Their governing parties, the Tigray People's Liberation Front (TPLF) and the Eritrean People's Liberation Front (EPLF), had different ideologies and organizational cultures. The EPLF, having won a thirty-year war for independence, was fiercely nationalistic and imbued with a powerful sense of self-reliance. The TPLF, now the core of the EPRDF coalition, was attempting to manage the complex ethnic politics of a vast and diverse federation. These divergent paths began to create economic and political strains.

The first major crack in the relationship appeared on the economic front. In November 1997, Eritrea decided to replace the Ethiopian birr and introduce its own national currency, the Nakfa. The move was a declaration of economic sovereignty, but it created an immediate and intractable crisis. Eritrea expected the two currencies to be exchanged at a one-to-one parity, allowing the seamless cross-border trade to continue. The Ethiopian government, however, viewed the situation differently. It argued that if the two were to be treated as separate national currencies, then all transactions between the two countries must be conducted in a hard, convertible currency, primarily the US dollar. This was a devastating blow to Eritrea, which lacked the foreign currency reserves to finance its trade with its much larger neighbor. Ethiopia's decision effectively brought the free trade arrangement to a grinding halt, choking the Eritrean economy and creating a climate of deep animosity.

Beneath the currency dispute lay a more fundamental and, as it would turn out, more explosive issue: the border. The thousand-kilometer-long boundary between the two nations was a colonial relic, a line drawn on maps by Italian and Ethiopian negotiators at the turn of the twentieth century. It had never been properly surveyed or physically demarcated on the ground. During the long years of the federation and the Derg regime, it was merely an internal administrative boundary, and local communities on both sides had for generations crossed it freely to farm, trade, and visit relatives. With the emergence of two sovereign states, this vague, invisible line suddenly became a matter of intense national importance. Both sides began to assert their claims more forcefully, printing new official maps that showed disputed territories as their own. Local administrators and militia from both countries began to engage in petty squabbles over tax collection and jurisdiction in the borderlands.

The flashpoint for this simmering dispute was a small, dusty, and otherwise insignificant market town called Badme. On May 6, 1998, a group of high-ranking Eritrean military officers leading a small patrol entered the Badme area, a region that was being administered by Ethiopia but was claimed by Eritrea. They were confronted by local Ethiopian police and militia units, who demanded that they disarm or leave. A tense argument erupted, and shots were fired. In the ensuing firefight, several of the Eritrean officers, including a unit commander, were killed.

The news of the killings was received in the Eritrean capital, Asmara, with fury. The government viewed the incident not as a local skirmish, but as a deliberate and premeditated act of aggression by Ethiopia. Rather than pursuing a diplomatic solution, President Isaias Afwerki opted for a massive and disproportionate military response. On May 12, 1998, just six days after the initial incident, Eritrea launched a full-scale, mechanized invasion. Several brigades of the Eritrean army, supported by tanks and heavy artillery, stormed across the border and seized control of Badme and the surrounding area. They quickly dislodged the lightly armed Ethiopian police and militia, establishing firm control over a significant swathe of territory.

In Addis Ababa, the initial Ethiopian reaction was one of stunned disbelief. The EPRDF government, preoccupied with its internal economic and political agenda, seemed to have been caught completely off guard. The sense of betrayal was profound. The brothers-in-arms, the allies who had fought and bled together, were now shooting at each other. As the news of the Eritrean occupation spread, a wave of nationalist outrage swept through Ethiopia. The public demanded a strong response, and the government, after a brief period of hesitation, was compelled to act. Prime Minister Meles Zenawi addressed the nation, condemning the invasion as a stab in the back and demanding the unconditional withdrawal of all Eritrean forces from Ethiopian territory. When Eritrea refused, the die was cast. Ethiopia began a massive mobilization of its army, and the border dispute escalated into a full-scale, conventional war.

The conflict that unfolded was unlike any other in the region's recent history. This was not the guerrilla warfare of the long struggle against the Derg. It was a brutal, positional war of a kind not seen since the Iran-Iraq War, a conflict eerily reminiscent of the Western Front in World War I. Both sides, led by commanders who had learned their craft in the same school of revolutionary warfare, poured hundreds of thousands of soldiers into three main fronts along the border. They dug vast, complex networks of trenches, bunkers, and machine-gun nests, creating formidable defensive lines that stretched for hundreds of kilometers.

The fighting was characterized by appalling attrition and human-wave assaults. In a series of major battles, tens of thousands of soldiers, often poorly trained conscripts, were ordered to charge across open ground into a hail of machine-gun and artillery fire. The casualties were staggering. Both nations, among the poorest on the planet, diverted their scarce resources to purchase sophisticated weaponry on the international market. The skies above the trenches became a new and terrifying battleground, as Ethiopian Sukhoi Su-27s and Eritrean MiG-29s, often flown by Russian and Ukrainian mercenaries, engaged in dogfights and bombed each other's positions. The air war also brought the conflict directly to civilians. In June 1998, an Eritrean air raid on the Tigrayan capital of Mekelle struck a primary school, killing dozens of children and teachers. The Ethiopians retaliated with air strikes on the airport in Asmara. The attacks horrified the world and hardened the resolve on both sides, making a negotiated settlement even more difficult.

International mediation efforts began almost immediately, led by a group of African heads of state under the auspices of the Organization of African Unity (OAU), with strong backing from the United States and the United Nations. The core of their peace proposal was simple: a ceasefire, Eritrean withdrawal to the positions held before the conflict began, the deployment of neutral observers, and the demarcation of the border by a neutral commission. For nearly two years, this basic framework was the subject of intense but fruitless shuttle diplomacy. The sticking point remained the same. Ethiopia, under its prime minister Meles Zenawi, refused to negotiate until Eritrea withdrew from every inch of territory it had occupied since May 1998. Ethiopia demanded a return to the *status quo ante bellum* as a precondition for talks. Eritrea, under President Isaias Afwerki, refused to countenance what it saw as a humiliating withdrawal without a prior, ironclad guarantee of a binding border demarcation process. The war settled into a long and bloody stalemate, punctuated by periodic, murderous offensives that achieved little but added tens of thousands to the death toll.

During this period of stalemate, both governments also turned on the civilian populations of the other country living within their borders. In a policy that was widely condemned as a violation of international humanitarian law, the Ethiopian government began the systematic deportation of tens of thousands of Eritreans and Ethiopians of Eritrean descent. Many of these people had lived in Ethiopia for generations, were Ethiopian citizens, and had no connection to the Eritrean state. They were rounded up, had their property confiscated, and were bussed to the border, often with only what they could carry. It was a campaign that ripped families apart and destroyed a vibrant and long-established community. Eritrea retaliated by expelling thousands of Ethiopian nationals from its territory.

By the spring of 2000, Ethiopia's patience had run out. After two years of stalemate, and having used the time to build a massive, well-trained, and well-equipped army of over 300,000 soldiers, Meles Zenawi decided to end the war with a final, decisive military blow. On May 12, 2000, Ethiopia launched Operation Sunset, a massive, multi-pronged offensive on the western Badme front. The Ethiopians had learned the lessons of the costly frontal assaults. This time, they used their overwhelming numerical superiority to bypass the main Eritrean trench lines, punching through weaker points in the defense and executing a classic pincer movement. The Ethiopian army poured deep into western Eritrea, capturing the strategic town of Barentu and cutting off the main Eritrean forces from their supply lines. The heavily fortified Eritrean front, which had been considered impregnable, collapsed with stunning speed.

Facing a complete and catastrophic military defeat, with Ethiopian columns advancing deep into its territory and threatening the road to the capital, the Eritrean government had no choice but to concede. Isaias Afwerki informed the OAU that he would now accept their peace plan, the very plan he had rejected for two years. With the fighting still raging, both sides signed a Cessation of Hostilities agreement in Algiers on June 18, 2000. This was followed by a comprehensive peace treaty, the Algiers Agreement, which was formally signed by Meles and Isaias on December 12, 2000. The war was officially over.

The Algiers Agreement established a framework for a lasting peace. It called for the withdrawal of all troops, the establishment of a 25-kilometer-wide Temporary Security Zone (TSZ) on the Eritrean side of the border, which would be monitored by a UN peacekeeping force (the United Nations Mission in Ethiopia and Eritrea, or UNMEE), and, most critically, the creation of an independent Eritrea-Ethiopia Boundary Commission (EEBC). This commission, based at the Permanent Court of Arbitration in The Hague, was mandated to "delimit and demarcate the colonial treaty border based on pertinent colonial treaties (1900, 1902 and 1908) and applicable international law." Both Ethiopia and Eritrea solemnly pledged in the agreement that the commission's decision would be "final and binding."

The cost of the war had been catastrophic. While precise figures are unknown, it is estimated that between 70,000 and 100,000 soldiers on both sides were killed, with many more wounded. The conflict had devastated the economies of both nations, diverting billions of dollars from development into destruction. But with the signing of the Algiers Agreement and the arrival of the blue-helmeted peacekeepers, there was a sense of cautious hope that the bloody and seemingly pointless conflict was finally at an end, and that the border question that had sparked it would now be resolved once and for all by the rule of law.

In April 2002, after months of deliberation, the EEBC in The Hague delivered its verdict. The ruling was a complex and detailed legal judgment, drawing the line based on its interpretation of the old colonial treaties. It awarded territory to both sides, splitting disputed areas in a way that defied the maximalist claims of either government. The crucial, symbolic decision, however, was on the status of the town of Badme. After meticulously analyzing the treaty texts, the commission awarded the town to Eritrea.

Initially, the Ethiopian government announced that it accepted the ruling. However, as the political implications of ceding the very town that the war had ostensibly been fought over began to sink in, Prime Minister Meles Zenawi's position began to shift. He soon declared that while Ethiopia accepted the ruling "in principle," the decision on Badme was "unjust" and a "blatant miscarriage of justice." He refused to allow the physical demarcation of the border to proceed until his concerns were addressed through further dialogue.

For Eritrea, this was the ultimate act of bad faith. President Isaias Afwerki insisted on the letter of the Algiers Agreement. The ruling was "final and binding," and there was nothing to discuss. He demanded that Ethiopia withdraw its troops from all territories awarded to Eritrea, including Badme, so that the physical demarcation could begin. The diplomatic process ground to a halt. Ethiopia refused to withdraw, and Eritrea refused to talk. The UN peacekeepers remained in their buffer zone, but their mission was effectively paralyzed. The war had ended, but the peace had been lost. The two nations entered a long, tense, and bitter standoff, a state of "no war, no peace" that would poison their relationship and destabilize the Horn of Africa for nearly two more decades.

CHAPTER TWENTY-FOUR: Ethiopia in the 21st Century: Growth, Challenges, and Transformation

The dawn of the new millennium found Ethiopia in a state of grim paradox. It was a victor, having decisively won the final, bloody battles of the war against Eritrea. Yet it was also a nation nursing a deep wound, its economy shattered and its people mourning tens of thousands of dead in a conflict that had ultimately solved nothing. The "final and binding" ruling of the international boundary commission, which awarded the symbolic town of Badme to Eritrea, was a political bombshell that Prime Minister Meles Zenawi refused to accept. The result was a bitter, frozen conflict—a state of "no war, no peace" that would define the region for nearly two decades. The border remained a heavily militarized trench line, and the two nations, once brothers-in-arms, settled into a long and hostile standoff, their armies staring at each other across an un-demarcated frontier.

This costly and inconclusive war triggered a political earthquake within the very core of the ruling party. The Tigray People's Liberation Front (TPLF), the senior partner in the EPRDF coalition, had been the architect of the new Ethiopia, but it was now tearing itself apart. A deep ideological fissure opened within its central committee. On one side was Prime Minister Meles Zenawi and his supporters, who argued that the war had exposed weaknesses in the party and that a more pragmatic, less hardline approach was needed. On the other was a faction of TPLF traditionalists, or "dissidents," who viewed Meles's handling of the war as a betrayal of Tigrayan interests and accused him of being too soft on Eritrea. The power struggle was fierce and secretive, a battle for the soul of the revolution fought behind closed doors. In March 2001, Meles emerged victorious. His key rivals were purged from the party, and some were later imprisoned on corruption charges. The split consolidated Meles's grip on power, transforming him from a first among equals into the undisputed master of both the party and the state.

With his internal authority secured, Meles embarked on the grand project that would define his legacy: the construction of a "developmental state." The theory, heavily inspired by the economic miracles of East Asian "tiger" economies like South Korea and Taiwan, was a radical departure from the Western liberal democratic model. It held that in a poor, agrarian country like Ethiopia, economic development must precede multi-party democracy. The state, guided by a disciplined and far-sighted ruling party, would be the primary driver of the economy, directing massive public investment into key sectors to achieve rapid, transformative growth. The goal was to build a powerful, centralized state capable of lifting millions out of poverty and turning Ethiopia into a middle-income country by 2025. It was a top-down, authoritarian vision of progress.

The developmental state went into action with breathtaking speed and scale. The government launched a series of five-year Growth and Transformation Plans, pouring billions of dollars into massive infrastructure projects. A web of new asphalt roads began to connect the country's remote regions. New universities sprang up in provincial towns. The most visible and ambitious symbol of this new era was the construction of the Grand Ethiopian Renaissance Dam (GERD) on the Blue Nile. Announced in 2011, the GERD was a project of immense national pride and strategic importance. It was to be the largest hydroelectric power plant in Africa, a mega-project financed almost entirely from domestic resources, including mandatory bond purchases from civil servants. The dam was a declaration of Ethiopia's ambition to become a regional powerhouse, but it also ignited a fierce diplomatic dispute with the downstream nations of Sudan and, especially, Egypt, which viewed any dam on the Nile as an existential threat to its water supply.

This state-led investment, coupled with significant foreign aid and investment, particularly from China, produced astounding results. For over a decade, Ethiopia's economy grew at a blistering pace, consistently ranking among the fastest-growing in the world. The official figures, often cited as being in the double digits, were a source of immense pride for the government. The skyline of Addis Ababa was transformed, with new skyscrapers, luxury hotels, and a modern light-rail system—the first of its kind in sub-Saharan Africa—testifying to a new era of prosperity. This narrative of an "African Lion" economy, of an "Ethiopian Renaissance," became the government's defining message to the world.

This economic boom, however, had a dark side. The developmental state was also a security state. The political space that had opened briefly in the early 1990s was systematically closed. Meles and the EPRDF viewed any form of organized political dissent not as a legitimate part of a democratic process, but as a dangerous threat to the stability required for their economic project. The press was muzzled, civil society organizations were neutered by restrictive laws, and opposition parties were harassed and marginalized.

The turning point came with the general election of May 2005. For the first time, a genuine and vibrant opposition movement was allowed to campaign with a degree of freedom. Two main opposition coalitions, the Coalition for Unity and Democracy (CUD) and the United Ethiopian Democratic Forces (UEDF), galvanized a huge wave of public support, particularly in the urban areas. On election day, the turnout was massive. As the first results began to trickle in, it became clear that the opposition, especially the CUD, was heading for a historic victory in Addis Ababa and had made significant inroads across the country.

Then, the government blinked. Claiming widespread irregularities, Prime Minister Meles Zenawi declared a state of emergency, banned all public demonstrations, and put the capital's election commission under his personal command. The CUD, crying foul and believing the election had been stolen, called on its supporters to protest. The government's response was brutal. In June, and again in November 2005, security forces opened fire on unarmed protesters in the streets of the capital, killing nearly two hundred people. In the aftermath, the entire leadership of the CUD, along with dozens of journalists and civil society activists, were arrested and charged with treason and attempting to overthrow the constitutional order. After a lengthy and highly publicized trial, many were sentenced to life in prison before being controversially pardoned and released in 2007. The message was clear and chilling: the EPRDF would not allow itself to be voted out of power. The brief, hopeful spring of Ethiopian democracy was over. In the next election in 2010, the EPRDF and its allies claimed an improbable 99.6 percent of the parliamentary seats.

While consolidating its rule at home, Ethiopia also began to assert itself as a regional hegemon, a role strongly encouraged by its new strategic partner, the United States. In the wake of the September 11th attacks, Washington came to view Ethiopia as a crucial and reliable ally in the global "War on Terror." The primary focus of this new alliance was Ethiopia's chaotic and stateless neighbor, Somalia. In 2006, a homegrown Islamist movement, the Islamic Courts Union (ICU), had brought a semblance of order to the Somali capital, Mogadishu, for the first time in over a decade. The ICU's rise, however, alarmed both Washington and Addis Ababa. The Ethiopians, with a long history of conflict with Somali nationalism and wary of the influence of radical Islam on their own large Muslim population, saw the ICU, particularly its hardline youth wing, al-Shabaab, as a direct threat to their national security.

With a green light and logistical support from the United States, the Ethiopian army launched a full-scale invasion of Somalia in December 2006. The powerful Ethiopian military quickly routed the ICU's militias and captured Mogadishu, installing the weak, UN-backed Transitional Federal Government. The intervention, however, proved to be a strategic disaster. The Ethiopian army found itself bogged down in a bloody and unwinnable urban guerrilla war against the remnants of the ICU, which had morphed into the far more radical and effective insurgency of al-Shabaab. The presence of the historic Christian enemy on Somali soil served as a powerful recruiting tool for the jihadists. After two years of costly occupation, the Ethiopian army withdrew in 2009, leaving behind a stronger, more radicalized al-Shabaab and a Somalia that was even more unstable than before.

In August 2012, the architect of this entire era, Prime Minister Meles Zenawi, died after a long illness. He had been the dominant figure in Ethiopian politics for twenty-one years, a leader who was hailed internationally as an intellectual giant and a visionary modernizer, but reviled by his opponents as a ruthless dictator. His death left a profound power vacuum. The EPRDF, a party that had been built around his personal and intellectual authority, now faced the challenge of managing a succession. In a carefully managed transition, the party leadership chose his deputy, Hailemariam Desalegn, to succeed him. Hailemariam was a stark contrast to his predecessor. He was not from the TPLF elite, but was a Wolayta from the diverse Southern Nations region. He was a soft-spoken technocrat, not a battle-hardened guerrilla leader. He pledged to continue Meles's policies, a philosophy that became known as the "Meles Zenawi vision."

For a few years, the system seemed to hold. The economic growth continued, and the apparatus of state control remained firmly in place. But without Meles's formidable authority to hold the fractious EPRDF coalition together, the deep-seated ethnic and political tensions that had been suppressed for years began to resurface with explosive force. The trigger was a seemingly innocuous urban planning document. In 2014, the government announced the "Addis Ababa Integrated Master Plan," a proposal to expand the administrative boundaries of the capital deep into the surrounding farmlands of the Oromia region.

For the Oromo people, Ethiopia's largest ethnic group, the plan was the final straw. They saw it as a land grab, a continuation of the historic process of marginalization that had seen their ancestral lands swallowed up by the expanding capital. The plan sparked a wave of mass protests that began in Oromia in late 2015 and quickly spread across the region. The protests were initially peaceful, but the government's response was, once again, brutal. Security forces used live ammunition against demonstrators, killing hundreds and arresting tens of thousands.

The brutal crackdown, however, did not quell the unrest; it inflamed it. The Oromo protests evolved from a single-issue demonstration into a full-blown popular uprising against the entire EPRDF system, which many Oromos viewed as a continuation of Tigrayan dominance. By 2016, the protest movement had spread to the Amhara region, the country's second-largest ethnic group. Here, the grievances were different—centered on disputes over administrative boundaries and a feeling of political and economic marginalization—but the target was the same: the TPLF-dominated regime. The unprecedented spectacle of the country's two largest ethnic groups, the Oromo and the Amhara, who had historically often been rivals, making common cause against the government shook the EPRDF to its core.

The government of Prime Minister Hailemariam Desalegn was flailing. He declared a state of emergency in October 2016, but the draconian measures failed to stop the protests. The developmental state, which had staked its legitimacy on delivering economic growth, was now facing a profound crisis of political legitimacy. The ethnic federalist system, which was supposed to have solved the "question of nationalities," had instead produced powerful ethno-nationalist movements that were now challenging the very foundations of the state. The EPRDF, paralyzed by internal divisions, was breaking apart. The reformist wing of the coalition, particularly within the Oromo and Amhara constituent parties, recognized that the old model of repressive, top-down rule was no longer sustainable. They began to push for a radical change in leadership.

After months of intense and secretive internal struggle within the ruling coalition, Prime Minister Hailemariam Desalegn, in a stunning televised address on February 15, 2018, announced his resignation. He stated that he was stepping down to allow for political reforms that could bring a lasting peace. His resignation set the stage for a dramatic leadership contest within the EPRDF. In April 2018, the coalition's council elected a new chairman, who would automatically become the next Prime Minister. Their choice was a young, charismatic, and enigmatic Oromo politician named Abiy Ahmed. He was a former army intelligence officer with a

PhD in peace and conflict studies, a man who had risen through the ranks of the Oromo wing of the party. He was swept to power on a tidal wave of popular expectation, a figure who seemed to promise a break from the repressive past and a new, more inclusive future. As he took the oath of office, a wave of what became known as "Abiymania" swept the country. Ethiopia, teetering on the brink of collapse, held its breath, waiting to see if this new leader could heal the deep divisions that were tearing the nation apart.

CHAPTER TWENTY-FIVE: The 2020 Civil War and the Quest for a Lasting Peace

The ascent of Abiy Ahmed to the office of Prime Minister in April 2018 was greeted with a surge of euphoric optimism not seen in Ethiopia for generations. A young, charismatic Oromo leader from within the ruling EPRDF coalition, he seemed to embody the promise of a new beginning. In his inaugural address, he electrified the nation with a message of unity, forgiveness, and hope, speaking of a new Ethiopian identity, *medemer*, or "synergy." The early months of his premiership were a whirlwind of dizzying and radical reforms. He ordered the release of thousands of political prisoners, unbanned opposition parties and armed groups that had been designated as terrorist organizations, and lifted draconian restrictions on the press. The air in Addis Ababa, long thick with fear and suspicion, was suddenly filled with the scent of freedom.

The most spectacular and internationally celebrated of these early moves was the sudden and complete rapprochement with Eritrea. For two decades, the two nations had been locked in a bitter and costly "no war, no peace" stalemate. In June 2018, Abiy announced that Ethiopia would fully and unconditionally accept the Algiers Agreement and the 2002 boundary commission ruling, the very decision his predecessor had rejected. A month later, in a historic visit to Asmara, he embraced President Isaias Afwerki. The scenes of the two leaders laughing and holding hands, and of the joyous public celebrations in both capitals, were broadcast around the world. Telephone lines were reconnected, flights resumed, and the border was officially reopened. For this dramatic act of peacemaking, Abiy Ahmed was awarded the 2019 Nobel Peace Prize. It seemed a confirmation of a new, hopeful chapter for the entire Horn of Africa.

This initial wave of "Abiymania," however, soon collided with the complex and deeply entrenched realities of Ethiopian politics. The very reforms that opened up the political space also unleashed powerful and often competing ethno-nationalist forces that had been suppressed for decades. Old border disputes between regional states flared into violent conflict, and millions of people were displaced by inter-communal violence. Abiy's philosophy of *medemer*, which called for a pan-Ethiopian national unity, was viewed with deep suspicion by many who had benefited from the ethnic federalist system. They saw it as a dangerous return to the centralized, assimilationist empire of the past.

The most formidable opposition to Abiy's new agenda came from the Tigray People's Liberation Front (TPLF). The TPLF, which had been the dominant force in the EPRDF coalition and the undisputed master of Ethiopia for twenty-seven years, found itself suddenly and decisively marginalized. Its powerful leaders were removed from key positions in the federal government and the military, and a new narrative took hold that blamed them for all the corruption and repression of the previous era. For the TPLF leadership, who had retreated to their regional stronghold in Mekelle, this was a humiliating and unacceptable reversal of fortune. They saw Abiy's reforms not as a genuine democratization but as a power grab designed to dismantle the federal system they had created and to destroy them as a political force.

The breaking point came in late 2019, when Prime Minister Abiy moved to dissolve the EPRDF coalition, a front of four ethnically-based parties, and replace it with a single, unified national party, the Prosperity Party. Three of the four constituent parties agreed to merge into the new entity. The TPLF flatly refused. They condemned the move as illegal and unconstitutional, a betrayal of the federalist principles upon which the state was founded. With this refusal, the TPLF was no longer part of the ruling establishment; it was now an opposition party, ruling its own region in open defiance of the federal government.

The political standoff escalated dramatically throughout 2020. A national election scheduled for August was postponed by the federal government, citing the public health risks of the COVID-19 pandemic. The TPLF accused Abiy of using the pandemic as a pretext to illegally extend his term in office. In a direct act of defiance, the Tigray regional government announced it would proceed with its own regional elections in September, in violation of the federal electoral board's ruling. The federal government declared the Tigrayan election illegal, and in return, the newly "elected" Tigrayan government declared that it no longer recognized the legitimacy of the federal government, whose mandate, they argued, had expired. The two sides were now locked in a cycle of mutual delegitimization. The federal government began to withhold budgetary funds from Tigray, and the TPLF blocked the appointment of a new head for the federal army's Northern Command, which was headquartered in Mekelle. The rhetoric grew increasingly bellicose, and both sides began to mobilize their forces.

The long-simmering political crisis finally exploded into open warfare on the night of November 3, 2020. In a televised address to the nation, Prime Minister Abiy announced that TPLF forces had launched a surprise, "treasonous" attack on the headquarters of the Ethiopian National Defense Force's (ENDF) Northern Command in Mekelle and on other federal military bases across the Tigray region. He stated that the TPLF had "crossed a red line" and that the government was being forced to undertake a military "law enforcement operation" to restore order and bring the "criminal clique" of the TPLF to justice. The TPLF leadership countered that their actions were a "preemptive self-defense" against an imminent federal invasion that they claimed was being coordinated with troops from neighboring Eritrea.

The initial phase of the war was swift and brutal. The federal army, alongside allied Amhara regional special forces and, crucially, troops from Eritrea who had secretly crossed the border from the north, launched a multi-pronged invasion of Tigray. Despite fierce resistance, the combined forces, with their overwhelming superiority in numbers and heavy weaponry, pushed the Tigrayan forces back. The federal government imposed a total communications blackout on the region, cutting off all internet and phone services and making it impossible for journalists to report on the conflict. On November 28, 2020, just three weeks after the war began, Prime Minister Abiy announced the capture of the regional capital, Mekelle. He declared that the law enforcement operation was over and that federal forces were now engaged in a manhunt for the fugitive TPLF leadership.

The reality on the ground, however, was far from the clean, swift operation the government had portrayed. The war had entered a new and horrific phase. For the next seven months, the people of Tigray were subjected to a reign of terror. Widespread and credible reports emerged of indiscriminate shelling of civilian areas, extrajudicial killings, and massacres of unarmed civilians by ENDF, Eritrean, and Amhara forces. The historic city of Aksum became the site of a particularly gruesome massacre, where Eritrean soldiers were reported to have systematically killed hundreds of civilians over a period of several days. Sexual and gender-based violence was used as a deliberate and systematic weapon of war, with countless women and girls subjected to horrific gang rapes and sexual mutilation. The region's infrastructure was systematically dismantled and looted. Factories were stripped, hospitals and schools were destroyed, and ancient monasteries were pillaged. A man-made famine began to take hold as invading forces burned crops, killed livestock, and deliberately blocked the delivery of humanitarian aid.

While the government in Addis Ababa insisted that life was returning to normal in Tigray, a dramatic reversal was taking shape in the rugged mountains of the region. The TPLF leadership had not been captured. They had escaped the fall of Mekelle and had successfully regrouped in the countryside. They reorganized their forces, which were now swelled by thousands of young Tigrayans enraged by the atrocities, under a new banner: the Tigray Defense Forces (TDF). In June 2021, after months of guerrilla warfare, the TDF launched a stunning counter-offensive codenamed Operation Alula. In a series of lightning attacks, they routed the ENDF divisions that were occupying the region. On June 28, 2021, the TDF marched back into Mekelle, sending the federally appointed interim administration fleeing in disarray. The Ethiopian government, in a face-saving gesture, declared a "unilateral humanitarian ceasefire" and withdrew the remainder of its army from most of Tigray.

The war, however, was far from over. It was about to enter an even wider and more dangerous phase. The TDF, feeling betrayed by the international community's failure to end the de facto humanitarian siege on their region, decided to take the war beyond Tigray's borders. They launched a new offensive, pushing south and east into the neighboring Amhara and Afar regions. The stated goal was to break the humanitarian blockade and to force the government in Addis Ababa to the negotiating table. The TDF also announced a formal military alliance with the Oromo Liberation Army (OLA), an insurgent group that had been fighting the federal government in the Oromia region. By October 2021, this new TDF-OLA alliance had captured the strategic cities of Dessie and Kombolcha on the main highway leading to the capital. Their forces were now within 200 kilometers of Addis Ababa.

The apparent threat to the capital created a wave of panic, both domestically and internationally. Foreign embassies began to evacuate their staff, and the government in Addis Ababa, facing a genuine existential threat, declared a national state of emergency. Prime Minister Abiy Ahmed, clad in military uniform, announced that he was going to the front lines to personally direct the war effort. A massive, nationwide mobilization was launched, with tens of thousands of ordinary citizens joining regional militias and the regular army to defend the capital. The government also made a crucial strategic decision: it rapidly acquired a fleet of sophisticated combat drones from foreign suppliers, including Turkey, the United Arab Emirates, and Iran.

The introduction of these armed drones proved to be the decisive turning point in the war. The TDF, a force that had been organized for infantry warfare in mountainous terrain, had no effective defense against this new threat from the air. Their long, exposed supply lines were systematically targeted and destroyed. Their troop concentrations were hit with devastating precision. The tide of the war turned as quickly as it had in June. The TDF-OLA advance on the capital was halted and then reversed. By December

2021, a major government counter-offensive had pushed the Tigrayan forces out of the Amhara and Afar regions and back into Tigray. The war settled into another grim stalemate, but the humanitarian catastrophe inside Tigray, which remained under a complete blockade, deepened to catastrophic levels.

For the next ten months, the stalemate held. Sporadic fighting continued, and the humanitarian crisis worsened, but both sides, exhausted by the carnage and facing mounting international pressure, began to tentatively explore the possibility of a negotiated settlement. The African Union, led by the former Nigerian president Olusegun Obasanjo, took the lead in a painstaking diplomatic effort to bring the warring parties to the table. After several false starts, formal peace talks between delegations from the Ethiopian federal government and the TPLF finally began in Pretoria, South Africa, in late October 2022.

The negotiations were tense and difficult, but after ten days of intensive talks, a breakthrough was announced. On November 2, 2022, the two sides signed a landmark agreement for the "Permanent Cessation of Hostilities." The Pretoria Agreement was a comprehensive pact to end the two-year-long war. The TPLF agreed to a complete and orderly disarmament, demobilization, and reintegration of its fighters. In return, the federal government agreed to lift the terrorist designation on the TPLF, to halt its military operations, and, crucially, to facilitate immediate and unhindered humanitarian access to the Tigray region. The agreement also called for the restoration of federal authority in Mekelle and the withdrawal of all foreign and non-ENDF forces from the region—a clear reference to the Eritrean army. A follow-up agreement on implementation was signed in Nairobi a week later.

The signing of the Pretoria Agreement was met with a profound sense of relief, both within Ethiopia and around the world. The guns fell silent, and for the first time in two years, a fragile peace began to take hold. Humanitarian aid started to flow back into Tigray, and essential services like banking and telecommunications were slowly restored. The war, which had killed hundreds of thousands of people, displaced millions, and brought the nation to the brink of collapse, was finally over. The path forward, however, remained fraught with immense challenges. The question of accountability for the horrific atrocities committed during the war was left unaddressed. The presence of Eritrean and Amhara forces in parts of Tigray remained a volatile issue. The deep political and ethnic fissures that the war had exposed had not been healed. The quest for a lasting peace, for reconciliation, and for the rebuilding of a shattered nation had only just begun.

Printed in Dunstable, United Kingdom